LEAVE A LEGACY

Reflections on the Strategies
of Great Leadership

Captain R. Stewart Fisher, USN, Ret.

SIGNALMAN PUBLISHING

Leave a Legacy
Reflections on the Strategies of Great Leadership
by R. Stewart Fisher

Signalman Publishing
www.signalmanpublishing.com
email: info@signalmanpublishing.com
Kissimmee, Florida

© Copyright 2014 by R. Stewart Fisher. All rights reserved. No part of this book may be reproduced or transmitted in any form or by any means, electronic or mechanical, or incorporated into any information retrieval system, electronic or mechanical, without the written permission of the copyright owner.

ISBN: 978-1-940145-18-1

Library of Congress Control Number: 2014932682

Dedicated to our loving God, family, children, grandchildren, and future generations.

Contents

Foreword................................9
Acknowledgments..........................13
Introduction............................17

I. Self Mastery 21

Strive for Excellence, Not Perfection.............. 23
"The Troll That Sits Under the Bridge" 24
Don't Show Off................................25
Don't Fake It................................. 26
Say, "I Was Wrong," and Mean It................27
Say, "I Don't Know," and Begin Learning..........28
Never Compare Yourself to Others 29
Seek Recognition for Others 30
Take Time to Reflect........................... 30
Even Heroes Have Warts 31
Use Your Wisdom to Be a Mentor 32
Listen and Then Make Courageous Decisions.......33
"Courage is Fear Hanging On for One Minute Longer"
.... 34
Have the Courage to Follow Your Own Path....... 35
Practice Self-Awareness......................... 36
The Power of Awe and Aha 37
Understand the Value of Patience 38
Stay within Your Range of Effectiveness 39
Seek Balance in Your Life 40
Unwind and Recharge Your Batteries 41
Live in the Present Moment 42
Don't Let Others Define You 43
Seize the Day................................. 44
Laugh at Yourself............................. 44
Be a Perpetual Learner 45

Be a "Rookie" with a Purpose 46
Don't Fear Being a "Work in Progress" 47
Learn the Lesson of the Sword 47

II. Improving Interactions 49

Follow the "Golden Rule" 51
Remember, "No Man is an Island" 51
You're Never Alone............................52
Lift Up Everyone You Meet 53
Be Kind to Strangers........................... 53
Love Them Anyway 54
Don't Expect the Scales to Balance 55
"Evil Triumphs When Good Men Do Nothing".....56
Don't Let Evil Discourage You 57
Don't Take It Personally..........................58
Take a Stand 59
Make a Difference...............................59
Understand the Power of Forgiveness............. 60
Forget About It 61
Nothing Happens in a Vacuum 62
Recognize the Unsung Heroes 62
Acknowledge Your Benefactors 64
Be Ready to Throw a Life Ring 64
Seek Respect, Not Popularity 65
Use the Power of Words 66
Never Underestimate the Power of a Kind Word ... 67
Teach and Share Knowledge 68
See the Good in People 68
Remember, You Can't Do It Alone 69

III. Optimum Team Leadership 71

Promote and Value Teamwork 73
Create Winning Teams 74

Be a Servant Leader 75
Understand the Value of Incentives 75
Set the Example..................................77
Value and Promote Friendship 77
Believe in Your Intuition 78
Listen! 79
Communicate!...................................80
Let Go 81
Use Stories and Analogies to Communicate........83
Recognize Leadership at All Levels................84
Beware the Abuse of Power 85
Calm Seas Do Not Make Good Sailors.............86
Take Note of Your Surroundings, Then Act........86
Pay Attention to Details 87
Sports Can Teach Life Lessons 88
Swing for the Fences 89
Just Shoot the Ball 90
Get up off the Mat and Never Give Up............91
Hustle Cures Anxiety 92
Keep Your Eye on the Ball 93
Give It Your Best Shot 94
Recognize Blind Alleys 95
Find Order in Chaos 96
Recognize the Value of Mistakes 97
Face Fear with Courage..........................98
Burn Your Ships 99
Don't Fear the Great Leap 100
Let Failure Empower You 101
Expect a Positive Outcome 101
Dare to Dream of Possibilities 102
Expand the Box and Explore New Ways...........103
Keep Moving Forward 105
Know When to Compromise 106
Pursue "Chudo" 106

"Shodo-O-Seisu" 107
"Shoshin-Ni-Kaeru" 108
Strive for "Dochu-No-Sei" 109

IV. Leave a Legacy and a Legion of Future Leaders
....111

Emphasize Character, Not Personality.............. 113
Let Your Spirit Shine 114
Seek "Masa-Katsu-Agatsu" 114
Steer by Your Stars.............................116
Believe in the "Spirit" of Leadership 116
Act According to Your Conscience 118
Recognize a Higher Power 119
Don't Seek Earthly Rewards 120
"To Thine Own Self Be True..." 121
Spread the Light 122

Appendix..124
Index...130
About the Author............................... 135

FOREWORD
from Coach John Wooden

Captain Stew Fisher's second book, *Leave a Legacy: Reflections on the Strategies of Great Leadership*, is another outstanding effort and a great companion to his and Captain Perry Martini's *Inspiring Leadership: Character and Ethics Matter*.

In his new book, Stew reveals the secrets great leaders have known throughout the ages: *Inspiring leadership comes from the heart, not the head.* Too often, however, the leadership we see being used today focuses on "management techniques" and totally misses what true leadership really is.

While being organized and efficient is certainly commendable, too many "managers" treat it like the Holy Grail. A true leader, however, realizes that the so-called soft stuff—such as friendship, loyalty, care, and concern—is really much more important in inspiring people to their greatest achievements. We are reminded of the old naval saying, "Take care of your sailors, and they will take care of the ship."

Stew points out that great leaders are humble. While they may have extraordinary talents and charisma, they turn the spotlight away from themselves and focus it on their people. They never feel a need to show off or engage in a contest of egos. Their sole purpose is to use their talents and experience to benefit those they lead.

They are masters of the concept of "servant leadership," always putting others before themselves. They know that others on their team often have talents or special skills that far exceed their own, so they let them shine. Great leaders are so well grounded and secure that they never worry about being eclipsed by a brighter light. They know when to be the teacher, and when to be the student—and expect to learn from everyone they meet.

Stew tells us that great leaders spend their entire lifetimes working on self-improvement. They certainly can't lead others until they have mastered themselves. They lead by example and adhere to the highest standards of conduct.

Stew points out that inspiring leaders see mistakes for what they really are: wonderful opportunities for growth and learning. They know that success is usually the last event in a long line of failures. They realize that they themselves are certainly not perfect, so why should they hold others to an impossible standard.

They seek *excellence*, but not *perfection*. All that really matters is that everyone has done his best. True leaders inspire their teams by telling them that they will cherish and share for a lifetime the memories of great achievement, but that mediocrity never leads to fulfillment and is quickly forgotten.

Leave a Legacy: Reflections on the Strategies of Great Leadership tells us that inspiring leaders seek balance in their own lives and for the people they lead. They constantly work to enhance body, mind, and spirit, knowing these are the three pillars for a fulfilling life. They are fun to be around and are able to laugh easily at their own human foibles.

Stew has written another marvelous book that captures the "true essence" of great leadership and resonates with the themes in my own books, especially *Wooden: A Lifetime of Reflections On and Off the Court.* The principles Stew and I both learned in the Navy reaffirm those that my dad, Joshua Wooden, taught me so many years ago on our Indiana farm. They apply in both military and civilian life, in all ages, and across all cultures.

Leave a Legacy: Reflections on the Strategies of Great Leadership is a timeless and wonderful book that you will want to keep on the shelf and refer to often. It explores the very same principles I used in my long coaching career at UCLA, and more importantly, as a father and a husband. It's another great read!

ACKNOWLEDGMENTS

I always admired UCLA Coach John Wooden for his strength of character and strong moral leadership. In a conversation I had with him before he died, I discovered that we shared a mutual admiration for many of the same leaders: the Good Lord, Abraham Lincoln, Mother Teresa, Martin Luther King, John F. Kennedy, and Robert E. Lee.

Coach Wooden graciously agreed to write the foreword for my book, and for that I am eternally grateful. We encounter leaders like Coach Wooden once in a generation. To share time with him was a rare privilege and one I'll never forget. I knew I was in the presence of greatness.

John Donne was so right when he said, "No man is an island." We are all touched by many people in our lives. My only fear is that I might leave someone out who truly deserves to be mentioned.

It should come as no surprise that I thank Audrey and Robert Fisher, my mom and dad, and Dr. John Fisher and Marian Kunz, my brother and sister, for their love and encouragement over all these years. My mom was an "Irish tiger" when it came to defending her kids.

My Godmother, Aunt Ruth Macdonald, always kept me going with her words of encouragement. She's still an inspiration to me today, even though she passed away recently at age 100.

My uncle, Ben Ashcraft, was a great role model. Whenever he would see me beating myself up over some mistake I had made, he would simply ask, "Well, did you learn something?" He made me realize that was all that really mattered in life: learning from our mistakes and moving on.

My cousins, Phil and Tinki Kilkeary, provided a welcome "port in a storm" during my days at Annapolis. They had a home just up the Severn River from the Academy and generously let me use their sailboat during June Week.

I also benefited from my grandparents' wisdom, and spent many hours listening to them over cups of coffee at the kitchen table. Later, when my granddad died, Norm Johanning filled that role and mentored me over many summers on Grand Traverse Bay in northern Michigan. I tagged along with him so much that he nicknamed me "Friday."

And who can forget those remarkable nuns at Sacred Heart Grade School and Saint Patrick's High who kept us on the "straight and narrow": Sisters Donata, Alicia, Jerom, Leonita, Marie Agatha, Marie Ouelette, and Paraclita. How they put up with us all those years I'll never know.

At the Naval Academy, I was blessed with many great friends: Colonel Hank and Beverly Richard, Captain Hendrix, Ron and Anne Spratt, Jim and Dianne Theis, Perry Martini, Mike Delbalzo, Bruce Gallemore, Garry Holmstrom, Craig Welling, Jim

Barron, Mark Horgan, Bill Hall, and Ross Dessert, to name just a few.

During the course of my career in the Navy, I served with many fine officers and sailors whose influence is felt to this day: Mac McLaughlin, Gene Pellerin, Steve Arends, Maury Docton, Lindsay Blanton, Chuck Erickson, Rick Haupt, Ray Hann, Dick Thomson, Gary Glashauser, Steve Keith, Dave Johnson, Bob Peyton, Bob Brockmeier, George Kokkinakis, Gene Mappin, Steve Jordan, Ken Comer, Mike Lambert, Rick Coyle, Dan Pinkerton, Larry Hayes, Paul Heron, Mary Jo Cervantes, Joe Aldridge, Tom Turnbull, and so many more. It was an honor and a privilege to serve with them.

In putting together this book, a renowned leadership consultant in her own right, Michele Jackman, was a great friend and mentor. She was instrumental in helping me with the outline and organization of the material.

Last, but certainly not least, my wife, Yolanda, has been my rock, providing me with love and support. And I was blessed with four great children, now in their 30s: Molly, Kelly, Patrick, and John. They made me want to become a better man so that I could be a better father. I never fully reached that goal, but I'm still trying.

Introduction

Leave a Legacy: Reflections on the Strategies of Great Leadership was actually the first book I wrote. I had just completed the manuscript in February of 2003 when my good friend and classmate from the Naval Academy, Captain Perry Martini, called me on the phone and said, "Stew, we should write a book together."

I told him I had just completed a rough draft of one, but I would be happy to put it on the back burner in order to collaborate with him on what became *Inspiring Leadership: Character and Ethics Matter*, published in November of 2004.

Now, after all these years, I felt it was time to go back to work on *Leave a Legacy.* Even though it had been in hibernation, so to speak, it still influenced many of my thoughts in *Inspiring Leadership*.

From my earliest days, I have always been a student of leadership. I guess it started in grade school when I was elected president of my fourth grade class. Anyone who attended parochial schools in the 1950s can probably relate to those formative years.

One of the duties of the class president was to come to the front of the room and keep order whenever "the good sister," a Catholic nun, left the room. The president was required to write the names of "kids who talked" on the blackboard, a thankless task and certainly not one to enhance your popularity.

Needless to say, when it came time to elect a new president for the second semester, Stew Fisher lost, <u>in a landslide</u>, to Ken Ray, an ignominious end to my early aspirations for political office. That was my first leadership lesson, and there were many more to come. (Humorous footnote: Ken Ray's popularity sank like mine as he dutifully wrote the names of various miscreants on the blackboard in the teacher's absence during that second semester. I guess he didn't learn from my mistake either.)

There have been many more leadership lessons during my time on the planet: camp counselor, senior class president, indoctrinating new plebes (freshmen) at the Naval Academy, Commanding Officer of a combat search and rescue squadron during Desert Storm, raising two daughters and two sons, to name a few. Each experience had something to teach me.

I also made a study of the great leaders in history to find out what made them so influential and inspiring: Hannibal, Alexander the Great, George Washington, Abraham Lincoln, Robert E. Lee, Teddy Roosevelt, Gandhi, John F. Kennedy, Mother Teresa, Martin Luther King, Ronald Reagan, Coach John Wooden, and Pope John Paul II. Of course, the greatest of them all was Jesus Christ.

Over time, through real life experiences, observing inspirational leaders that I've known in action, and the study of great leaders before me, I developed my own leadership philosophy. Without a doubt, I probably learned the most from my own leadership mistakes.

There's no reason for any aspiring leader to make the same mistakes that I did. That is one of the principle reasons for writing this book, and I hope it will be of help to you as we explore the art of leadership together.

I will ask you many probing questions, the same ones I have asked myself over the years. The answers will allow you to reflect on your own leadership style and make the changes necessary to become a better leader. It's a lifelong process, but one that is truly worth the effort.

I
SELF MASTERY

Strive for Excellence, Not Perfection

The pursuit of perfection is neurotic, but striving for excellence is a worthy goal. Trying to be perfect only leads to frustration. You're human and therefore can never be perfect. But doing your best in all things leads to excellence.

"He who will not risk, cannot win." In expanding the envelope, you will experience many failures, but that's okay. Use every misstep as a learning experience. It is said that success is the last event in a long line of failures. But remember, all of mankind's greatest achievements were littered with many mistakes and failures along the way. Consider the Founding Fathers' initial attempts to write a Constitution, or our nation's long struggle for racial justice. How about the space program? In every one of those examples, failure always preceded success.

Has the fear of failure kept you from striving for excellence? Are you playing it safe, content to maintain the status quo? How much progress is possible if you do that? Learn the lesson of history: Success is achieved only by those who aren't afraid to fail.

"The Troll That Sits Under the Bridge"

Comedian Dennis Miller tells us, "Ego is the troll that sits under the bridge," waiting to ambush each of us. But we can learn an important lesson from the most influential men and women in history. Lincoln, Gandhi, Jesus, and Mother Teresa, to name just a few, all shared one important trait: *humility*. They preferred a place beside the common man. They never sought privileged status or entitlement.

Just as great rivers lie below the streams that feed into them, so do great men find their place as servant leaders. Their power and influence come from humility rather than pride. The Bible tells us that at the Final Judgment, "The first shall be last, and the last first." And it goes on to say, "Pride comes before the fall."

Ignore your press clippings. Don't build a trophy case. As soon as you begin to bask in your own accomplishments, you start to become self-important. You start to think of yourself as better than others, someone deserving special treatment. You become aloof, unable to relate to others. This separation will lead to your downfall because you've now set yourself apart from the team. Never forget, it was the team that got you where you are in the first place.

The talents that helped you succeed are only *gifts* of the Creator anyway. They were never *yours* in the first place, just something you were given at birth. They are meant to complement the gifts of others. Remember, "To whom much is given, much will be expected." That's why arrogance is really *an act of forgetting*, overlooking the true source of our inheritance.

How much time do you waste reading your own press clippings? Is ego getting in your way? Do you think your accomplishments were a solo effort? Has arrogance separated you from your team? Do you think you're somehow better than everyone else? Are you overly concerned with the perks of seniority, the big office, executive dining room, designated parking space, traveling first class?

We need to remind ourselves that deep down inside, we also have warts. While we may try to hide these faults from others or pretend they don't exist, we can't wish them away. When we're brutally honest with ourselves, we realize we have a lot to work on. There's much room for improvement. That fact alone should keep us humble.

Do you think you are perfect? Have you run out of things to improve upon? Then you haven't looked closely enough.

Don't Show Off

As we said, our talents were only meant to be used humbly, in the service of others. But sometimes it's tempting to strut your stuff and make a show of these gifts. When we do this, it's only because we've forgotten that our talents are on loan and were never really ours to begin with. *And they certainly weren't meant to be used to showcase ourselves.* Nothing is sadder than seeing someone who has been blessed with great gifts waste them, or worse, lord it over others.

Unfortunately, we see many examples of the misuse of God-given talent. For example, running backs showboating in the end zone after a touchdown, taking off their helmets as they preen in front of the cameras; defensive linemen taunting the quarterback after a vicious sack; basketball players trash talking with an opponent up and down the court.

Showing off is juvenile, arrogant, and totally lacking in sportsmanship. It is an abuse of talent and is merely exercising the ego. It is better to follow the example of Johnny Unitas, one of the NFL's greatest quarterbacks. After a phenomenal play, he merely trotted over to the sideline as if nothing extraordinary had happened. You'd never know, from his body language, that he had just thrown the winning touchdown.

How about you? Do you use your talents to help others, without fanfare? Or are you just showing off?

Don't Fake It

Being a chameleon only wears you out. It's impossible to be all things to all people. However, some of us still try to show the face we think people will like. But by trying to assume so many different identities, we forget who we really are.

Why do we do this? Often it's to fit in, or to save face. We're uncomfortable with who we are, so we assume false characters, rather than actually working on changing ourselves and becoming better people.

The solution: Forget what others think. Be yourself. It's a lot less work. Besides, true friends like you for who you are, warts and all, not who you pretend to be. That doesn't mean there's no room for improvement. But draw up *your own* blueprint for who you'd like to become. Don't let others do it for you.

Do you fake it in order to be accepted or to avoid self-improvement? Are you overly concerned what people think? Do you have a vision for the person you want to become? What are your daily goals to make those changes?

Say, "I Was Wrong," and Mean It

You're human. You're going to make mistakes. That's why you need to be able to say, "I was wrong," or, "I'm sorry." And it's better not to waste any time saying it.

Don't think by waiting things will get any better. Mistakes aren't like fine wines that improve with age. You may be trying to save face, or pretend you weren't at fault. But in the long run, it's better to come clean and put your error behind you rather than letting it fester.

Does pride prevent you from admitting you're ever wrong? Why would you think you're suddenly infallible? How is that attitude affecting your team?

If you can demonstrate a healthy attitude toward your own mistakes, you create the exact environment you're looking for on your team. People will know it's okay to fail. In fact, *failures become a measure of the number of courageous attempts you made*. In the long run, this is the only way to be successful.

Say, "I Don't Know," and Begin Learning

We often try to bluff our way through when we don't know an answer in order to save face or hide our ignorance. But the only thing that does is to pass on erroneous information which may cause our leaders to make bad decisions, often with tragic consequences, especially in wartime.

The words, "I don't know," from subordinates are honest and can be invaluable. They let leaders know where they stand, and when they need to seek more information. They establish the boundaries of ignorance and can then become the starting point for new knowledge. Knowing *what doesn't work* can be extremely beneficial. Just ask Thomas Edison, who tried hundreds of different materials for the filament in his electric light bulb, before discovering tungsten.

Is your team afraid of saying, "I don't know"?

Why? Do they fear retribution or looking bad? As a leader, what are you doing to change that? Remember, you must first establish an atmosphere of trust that will allow people to speak up and not feel foolish or worry about their jobs. You can start by saying, "I don't know," a few times yourself. Show that you're not the infallible master of all knowledge. That creates an honest environment for everyone else.

Never Compare Yourself to Others

When you compare yourself to others, there are two possible outcomes, *both bad*. You either become arrogant, thinking you're better than everyone else, or envious, jealous that you're not.

No two people on this earth are alike. Each of us has unique talents; each of us has his own faults. And ultimately, each of us has his own destiny and path to follow in life. No one of us is better than another. The great philosophers tell us that we're much like snowflakes: each unique, but all part of the same snowfall. We advance as human beings by supporting each other with our complementary talents, not by competing.

Do you waste your life's energy comparing yourself to others and being jealous or proud? Compare yourself only to the person you were yesterday, and seek to be a little bit better today.

Seek Recognition for Others

One of the most difficult things in life is to do good works without looking for accolades. We all have the need for recognition, to be acknowledged for what we've contributed or accomplished. Rare indeed is the man who can perform his service to others in total anonymity.

While that ideal is seldom achieved, it's still something to strive for. The Bible tells us that "those who seek their rewards on earth, have no need of rewards in heaven." But that's where the rewards will be much greater, if only we can postpone the need for public recognition today.

Are you able to serve others in total anonymity without thought of earthly rewards? Do you do good works for their own sake, or for the recognition they bring?

Take Time to Reflect

Every day, we seem to get bombarded by a never ending salvo of major and minor crises. We end up skipping lunch or a workout in order to devote more time to our growing backlog of work. It sometimes seems that the more hours we spend at our desks, the more behind we get.

However, a wise leader should put his feet up on the desk at least once a day and pause to reflect. Dim the lights and close your eyes. Relax, take a few deep breaths, and listen—internally. These quiet moments spawn creativity. This is when you, as a leader, develop and refine your vision. Without a creative vision you are not a leader, merely a manager of chaos, a fireman racing to the next alarm.

Do you, as a leader, take time to reflect every day? Do you have a vision for your team? Do you know where you're taking them, what you want them to be? Have you articulated your vision? Most importantly, do you live it by your example?

Even Heroes Have Warts

When we closely examine the lives of the great men and women in history, we discover that they had faults just like the rest of us. Rather than being marble statues, they had warts. In fact, that's what makes them so human and allows us to connect with them.

All of his life, Ben Franklin kept a journal of the many faults he was trying to overcome. He made daily entries of his progress. Abraham Lincoln could be very absent-minded and was a terribly permissive parent. Much to the dismay of Thomas Herndon, Lincoln's law partner, the future president's boys often made a mess of their law office as the young rascals ran around, totally out of control. Churchill had a terrible temper, and John F. Kennedy was a notorious womanizer.

However, because we can see that great leaders weren't perfect, but very human, we find them even more real. We honor and remember them because, in spite of their flaws, they rose to greatness and inspired us.

Do you allow your heroes to be human? Do you focus on their good qualities, but acknowledge that they had flaws like the rest of us? Can you see that makes them more real? Does their example allow you to worry less about being perfect?

Use Your Wisdom to Be a Mentor

We'd like to think that as we get older, we learn a few tricks along the way. It would be nice to take credit for this growing wisdom. In reality, most of it can be attributed to a lifetime of mistakes, and not some spectacular achievement on our part.

The fact remains, those mistakes were great teachers. Sometimes we had to be hit over the head a few times because we kept making the same mistakes. But hopefully, over time, we learned the lesson they were trying to teach us.

What's the point of all this? Simply, it's up to those who have lived on the planet a little longer to pass on what they've learned to the next generation. There's no reason why our kids must make the same mistakes we did. Hopefully, we can give them a head start, further up the learning curve.

Sure, there will be those who stubbornly insist on repeating our old mistakes for themselves, burning their hands on the stove, so to speak, in spite of our warnings. But for those willing to listen, we should save them that trouble and serve as mentors.

What are you doing to pass on what experience has already taught *you*? Are you using one of the best tools, your own example? Do you lose patience and give up at the first sign of resistance to your mentoring? Can you remember a time in your own life when you could be thick-headed and unwilling to listen?

Listen and Then Make Courageous Decisions

Many times I've been the pilot in command of a helicopter on a low level navigation flight. On one training mission, two of the crewmen and I agreed we were in a certain position, but the fourth crewman calculated a different position. We listened to his reasoning (which was based on what he saw from looking at the surrounding terrain). He pointed out terrain features we had missed. Sure enough, that one crewman was right, but we never would have gotten back on track if we had ignored him.

Eventually, you'll reach a point where it's time to decide. As Eisenhower realized before launching the D-Day invasion at Normandy, very few decisions are ever *absolute* certainties. Those aren't decisions anyway. They're *forgone conclusions*. They're easy to make. Where would be the leadership challenge in that? A tough decision, however, takes courage. Further waiting only results in a missed opportunity. As the Nike ad says, "Just do it."

Are you paralyzed by the fear of failure or the neurotic pursuit of perfection? But aren't you human? Aren't you going to make mistakes? Were any great achievements ever realized without many mistakes being made along the way?

"Courage is Fear Hanging On for One Minute Longer"

General Patton used to say that "courage is fear hanging on for one minute longer." Without fear there can be no courage. Without something to overcome, where would be the challenge?

A chief petty officer once said with humble honesty, "Skipper, I don't feel I have courage because I have feelings of fear." But courage is not the absence of fear; it is taking action *in spite of* your fear. People who act without feeling fear are only foolhardy, but certainly not courageous.

The greatest examples of courage are often not physical, but psychological. We all want to be popular, to be liked, to belong. Thus, we often seek popularity rather than respect. But frequently, taking a courageous stand requires risk, doing something that isn't popular, but right.

As a leader, do you encourage devil's advocates? Do you realize that they are demonstrating true courage and have far more to contribute to your team than yes men?

At great risk to themselves, they are telling you what you don't want to hear. How you respond to them sends a powerful message to your team. While you may find them annoying sometimes, you must show them respect and encourage their contrary opinions. Then others will know that they can speak out constructively as well, which is the healthy environment you want to have.

Have the Courage to Follow Your Own Path

Each of us has a unique path to follow in life. But sometimes we have difficulty even knowing what that path might be. It is only by trial and error, making a lot of mistakes along the way, that we discover our true calling. Once we find what that is, it then takes courage to follow it.

One thing is certain. We will fail many times. We will lose our way. But courage comes from getting back up again, dusting ourselves off, and moving forward.

True friends will come into our lives to help us stay on track. And there is a power beyond our understanding that helps us as well. But only one thing counts: *Have the courage to keep moving.*

Do you listen to your inner voice to guide you on your path? Having heard it, do you have the courage to follow it?

Practice Self-Awareness

Many of the greatest leaders in history were highly introspective.

Why is that an attribute of so many influential men and women? Simply, by knowing themselves, they had a better understanding and empathy for their fellow human beings and a greater insight into their own humanity. By discovering their own motivations, they learned how to motivate other people. By examining their own thoughts and feelings, they understood how others might think and how they might feel. They became much more aware of the common bond they shared. Because they were closely connected with those they led, they became powerful leaders.

In fact, empathy is one of *the* most important leadership attributes. It is gained by knowing ourselves deeply and listening to that inner voice of conscience when we deal with others. Therein lies the power of the Golden Rule, "Do unto others, as you would have them do unto you."

As a leader, how well do you know yourself? Are you able to look at yourself honestly, warts and all? Or do you delude yourself by somehow thinking you're better than the rest of humanity? Have you lost touch with what it means to be human? To have hopes, aspirations, emotions, longings, and most importantly, flaws? If so, how can you ever expect to lead anyone?

The Power of Awe and Aha

Never lose your capacity for awe. The ability to be amazed keeps you humble. It lets you acknowledge and appreciate wonders beyond your capability, knowledge, or control. Consider the infinite, expanding universe; the magical, hovering flight of the humming bird; or even the resilience of the tiniest life form existing at the bottom of the ocean. All should inspire awe.

The more we learn, the more we realize how little we really know. In fact, the length, breadth, and depth of our ignorance is astounding. Just when we humans were beginning to think of ourselves as the fountain of all knowledge, we discovered what a small place we really occupy in this universe. We were no longer the center of creation—actually far from it.

But that gives us a healthy perspective. While it humbles us, it should also ignite our curiosity for further discoveries in the infinite universe we inhabit.

Do you still retain a sense of wonder and awe? Or do you think there's nothing more to learn? Perhaps the only thing larger than the universe is our ignorance of it.

Understand the Value of Patience

Becoming a better leader has much in common with learning Aikido, learning to fly, or any other new skill. Often, progress comes in a series of breakthroughs, after weeks of seeming stagnation.

The human mind needs a gestation period to consolidate and process the many inputs that ultimately create a unified whole. Like planting, fertilizing, and then harvesting, it's a process that can't be rushed or abbreviated. Learning follows those same patterns of nature. Improvement will happen *when it happens*. Just enjoy the journey. There will be learning plateaus in anything new you attempt to master. But overall, when you look back, you'll see the progress you've made.

Comparing yourself to others will only frustrate you. We all have our eureka moments at different times, unique for each individual. Trust that your daily effort towards improvement works if you can just be patient. Strive to be a little better than you were the day before. Realize that even during those seeming periods of stagnation or regression, learning, growth, and improvement are actually going on.

As a leader, are you able to see improvement as a natural process, one that takes time and patience? Or do you expect an immediate harvest, without tilling and planting the soil first? Are your decisions short sighted, governed by the tyranny of the quarterly report? Or are you able to think strategically with your focus on long term goals? Do you take shortcuts just to look good now, but risk the long term health of the company? Do you invest time developing your future leaders, or do you do make *all* the decisions rather than take a chance that they'll make a mistake?

Stay within Your Range of Effectiveness

Stay within your range of effectiveness. This simply means maintain your balance; don't overreach. We remain much stronger and more stable that way.

When kayaking, if you reach too far with your paddle, you could capsize. If you devote all of your waking hours to work, your marriage and family will suffer. At the other extreme, if you spend all your free time driving kids to soccer, little league, band practice, ballet lessons, karate, movie theaters, and the mall, you'll also lose the proper balance in your life.

In corporate America, we see huge mergers and acquisitions, companies buying out other businesses far outside their areas of expertise. These large conglomerates usually fail miserably and become stumbling giants, ineffective because they are operating in business areas they really don't understand. Sony stumbled when it bought American golf courses and movie studios. Time Warner made a major mistake when it merged with AOL.

As a company do you "stick to the knitting," your area of expertise? Or do you mistakenly equate size with success, diluting your competence and losing your agility in the marketplace? As a parent, do you find a balance between devotion to your kids and the needs of you and your spouse? Or have you become your kids' adult slave?

Success in life or business requires balance and staying within your range of effectiveness.

Seek Balance in Your Life

Remember that you are body, mind, and spirit. All of these must be nourished. Neglect any one area, and the others suffer.

The bodily dimension is easy to understand. Eat the right foods and get enough rest and exercise. Challenge yourself physically, but don't overdue it. If you get injured, allow enough time to heal.

We also need mental stimulation. This may come through reading, crossword puzzles and brain teasers, writing our thoughts in a journal, or watching educational TV—but avoiding the mindless drivel that passes for entertainment.

Taking care of the spirit is not as well defined. It involves things such as humor and laughter, the enjoyment of music and art, meditation, watching a sunset, listening to waves breaking on a secluded beach, religious worship, service to others, being with friends and family. Often a favorite physical activity can have a spiritual dimension as well: skiing through deep powder, surfing the perfect wave, or kayaking down a scenic river.

Unless we recognize and nourish all three dimensions, we will be out of balance and incomplete as human beings.

Do you take care of your body, mind, and spirit? Are you overlooking any of these dimensions? Do you *make* time on your schedule for regular exercise, family, friends, quiet reflection, reading, and recreation? Do you realize that they are just as important to your well being and success as work?

Unwind and Recharge Your Batteries

Life is not a continuous sprint. Even NASCAR drivers know that they can't keep the pedal to the metal the entire race. They must pace themselves and their finely-tuned machines in order to finish.

Yet, we often insist on burning ourselves out, failing to take a needed break and unwind. In the long run, we do great physical, mental, and emotional damage to ourselves. We not only risk being able to complete the immediate task at hand, but more importantly, our life's work.

Easing off on the accelerator is absolutely necessary. Take a break and do something relaxing and enjoyable, even if it seems a frivolous waste of time. In truth, it's an investment in your own physical, mental, and emotional health. You'll quickly discover renewed energy. Your creativity will be released and your spirits will soar. In the long run, you'll accomplish far more than if you kept your nose to the grindstone without taking a break.

Do you allow time to recharge your batteries, or are you continually burning the candle at both ends? Would your team call you a slave driver? When was the last time you got away from the office together and just had some fun? When was the last company picnic? Were families invited? Do your people look tired? Are they leaving work in time to have dinner at home? What kind of hours are they keeping? Do you even know? Do you promote a physical fitness program? Or are the only benefits you offer monetary?

Live in the Present Moment

The here and now is really all we have. The past can't be brought back; the future hasn't arrived yet. Make the most of the present moment. Do your best—*right now*! It gives you the greatest chance of creating a better future.

There are no guarantees that all your efforts will pay off. But dwelling on past mistakes, or worrying about future ones, will surely rob you of your ability to perform well in the present. The errors of the past should only be used to educate you, not fill you with regret and guilt.

Do you waste energy feeling guilty about the past or worrying about the future? Are you able to focus on the present, the only thing you really have any control of? Do you demonstrate that attitude to those you lead?

Don't Let Others Define You

We often worry too much about what people think. In some cases, this can even paralyze us. We wonder, "Will I still be liked?" or, "Will they laugh at me?" We let the opinions of others dictate our behavior instead of just being ourselves.

We should measure ourselves only by our own Guiding Principles. Are we living up to them? Really, that's all that matters. Chasing this elusive person others want you to be is futile. You can never be *that* person. You can only be yourself.

True friends stand by you, no matter what. They accept you for who you are. False friends will wither away. And isn't it better to find out who they are sooner rather than later?

How much are you influenced by the opinions of others? Are they able to make you abandon your Guiding Principles just so that you'll fit in and be popular? You can never be all things to all people anyway. Be the person *you* want to be. Don't let others do that for you.

Seize the Day

Dr. Wayne Dyer once described the present moment as the sand passing through the center of the hourglass. This sand, the here and now, is really the only time within our control. The sand already at the bottom represents the past, ancient history. The sand at the top of the hourglass is the future, also beyond our control.

Regrets or feelings of guilt about the past are a waste of life's precious energy. The same is true of worrying about the future. Living well in the present moment should be our only focus. It is the secret to future happiness. Each of us is given the same 24 hours in a day. What we do with that 24 hours makes all the difference in the world.

Are you bogged down with regrets about the past? Are you spending needless time worrying about a future that hasn't arrived yet? Remember, that's stealing your ability to live life fully in the present.

Laugh at Yourself

We all take ourselves too seriously, forgetting that we're human and make mistakes. Rather than agonize over the discovery that you aren't perfect, try another approach: *Laugh at yourself.* Find humor in your absent-mindedness, bungled attempts at athletic prowess, silly ego-driven attempts to be the center of attention.

Being totally honest with yourself and your imperfections saves a lot of emotional energy. You no longer have to pretend you're something you're not. Be at peace with the person you are. That doesn't mean you give up on self-improvement, just that occasional setbacks don't throw you off balance. This will lead to a saner, happier life.

When was the last time you laughed at yourself? Do you cling to a need to be perfect? Does that pursuit even make sense? How is your neurotic perfectionism affecting your team? Has your pressure made them so anxious they are no longer creative and productive? If so, then it's time to lighten up.

Be a Perpetual Learner

Continuous learning should be a lifelong goal. The more we learn, the more we discover how little we really know. This is good because it keeps us humble. There is always more to learn, and hopefully, someone around to teach us. Leaders must realize their shifting roles: sometimes teachers, sometimes students. Acknowledge the brilliance that exists among subordinates. Everyone else is smarter in some way, often in many ways. The wise leader taps into the expertise of those around him. Feigning knowledge fools no one—except, perhaps, the leader himself!—and undermines the respect junior people have for the boss.

Do you have the attitude that everyone has something to teach you? Do you study the great leaders of history to find out what made them great? Do you read a lot? Do you avoid the mindless TV shows that offer neither education, inspiration, nor humor? Have you made being a perpetual learner a lifelong goal?

Be a "Rookie" with a Purpose

Never fear being a rookie. In any new, worthwhile endeavor, you have to accept the role of a beginner. Our egos are seldom comfortable with that, but don't let that stop you. Forge ahead anyway.

You're going to feel awkward, ill at ease, and probably foolish, especially if you compare yourself to others who are more accomplished. But recognize that you have your own path to follow. It is unique. As wise men tell us, "The journey of 1000 miles begins with the first step." Don't let your ego stop you from taking it.

Does your ego prevent you from attempting something new and difficult? Are you afraid of being called a rookie? Do you only stay within your area of expertise? Do you always have to be the boss, or can you give others the chance to lead? Can you play the role of a student, or be a good follower? Remember, anyone who hasn't learned to follow orders, should not be allowed to give them.

Don't Fear Being a "Work in Progress"

Life's journey is one of motion. If you stand still, you stagnate and eventually die.

Have you ever noticed what often happens to retirees who don't find a new pursuit? Within a year of two, they are often dead. Contrast that to Morihei Ueshiba, the greatest martial artist Japan has ever known. He practiced Aikido until the day he died at 86. His art was always growing, evolving, and improving.

In a lifetime, we can never achieve perfection. The most we can hope for is *increasing excellence*. Never stop moving forward. Seek new challenges. Attempt to master new and difficult areas. No one should ever *arrive* at a "destination," even in a lifetime.

Do you think you've arrived? Have you chosen to stagnate on a plateau? Have you and your team stopped growing, learning, and creating? If so, what are you doing to shake things up and seek the next challenge?

Learn the Lesson of the Sword

Have you ever watched a sword smith at work? He takes the rough and imperfect metal and fires it in the furnace. Then he pulls it out of the fire and pounds on it with a hammer to temper and harden it. Back in the furnace it goes. After a few minutes, it's taken out and hammered again. This process is repeated many more times until all the imperfections in the metal are pounded out. Only then has he created a sword to be proud of and worthy of his indelible stamp on the blade.

In a sense, we are all like that sword. We make our mistakes and must be put back in the furnace, then hammered to remove our imperfections. This process is repeated until the lesson is finally learned. Over time, after many mistakes, we become better human beings. That's the lesson of the sword.

Do you see your mistakes as the path to learning and excellence? Do you understand the lesson of the sword?

II

IMPROVING INTERACTIONS

Follow the "Golden Rule"

There's a good reason they call it the Golden Rule. If everyone followed that one premise, "Do unto others as you would have them do unto you," the world would be a better place for us all.

It's so simple. And yet how many times do we catch ourselves not following it? We often end up focusing on ourselves and our own selfish interests, as if we were alone in the world. We fail to appreciate the impact we have on others. But as the poet, John Donne, tells us, "No man is an island." What we do *does* affect other people. Ultimately, what hurts others will also hurt us; what helps others will help us. We "reap what we sow."

Do you follow the Golden Rule? Is it a part of your life's philosophy? Is it a norm for your team?

Remember, "No Man is an Island"

John Donne said, "Never ask for whom the bell tolls; it tolls for thee." What did he mean?

To understand, we must transport ourselves to England during that time, the 16th Century. Back then, nearly everyone lived in rural farming villages. The church was the tallest building in town, and the church bell rang out for all important events. When it tolled, it announced to all the villagers out in their fields that a death had occurred. But rather than asking, "Who died?" John Donne wants us to realize that the death of any villager really means that a part of the village has died as well, since we're all connected in our humanity.

So it is on any team. We rely on each other. A victory for one is a victory for all. As the signers of the Declaration of Independence said with gallows humor, "If we don't hang together, then they will surely hang us separately."

As a leader, does your team hang together? Do they feel connected? Or do you treat them like interchangeable parts in a machine, overlooking their shared humanity?

You're Never Alone

I strongly suspect that those who commit suicide have given in to total despair. They must feel terribly alone and without hope at the moment they take their own lives.

But every person walking the face of this earth is important. The loss of any one of us diminishes us all. Where there is life, there is always hope. Even the most despicable of men can turn his life around and become a force for good. The Bible tells us about Saul, on his way to Damascus to kill Christians. He was struck from his horse and became Saint Paul, one of Christianity's greatest saints.

I'm convinced that Jesus mourned the death of

his betrayer, Judas. Even if a man seemingly has no friends, there is a Higher Power who cares for him. That, in itself, is reason enough never to give up hope.

Do you ever give in to despair or a sense of abandonment? Is there someone you know who appears to have done so? What have you done to intervene? Your expression of caring and friendship may be the only thing that saves him.

Lift Up Everyone You Meet

Everyone who meets you should be better off because of it. Make that your goal. You may do it with a kind word, empathetic listening, or most powerfully, through your own example.

Decide right now to project positive energy to those around you. Be a force for good. Work on your own character traits in order to shine with a brighter mirror. People will see your light. Spread it as far as you can.

Are you a positive force for others? Are they better off for having known you? What kind of an example do you set? Would people want to emulate you? Do you inspire others?

Be Kind to Strangers

In their poor clothes, an elderly couple approached the President of Harvard University. "Our son loved Harvard in the year he attended," they told him, "but he was recently killed in an accident. We would like to donate money for a memorial to him."

The pompous president, who had already kept the couple waiting for several hours, replied gruffly, "Why, Madam, if we did that, this place would look like a cemetery." She replied, "Oh no, we don't want to erect a statue. We want to donate a building." The president, dismissing them because of their homespun attire, said, "Do you realize we have over half a million dollars invested in buildings here?"

The lady turned to her husband and said quietly, "Is that all it costs to start a university? Why don't we just start our own?" Her husband nodded.

The president's face wilted in confusion and bewilderment. Mr. and Mrs. Leland Stanford got up and walked away, traveling to Palo Alto, California, where they established the university that bears their name, a memorial to a son that Harvard no longer cared about.

How do you treat the "little people" you encounter? Do you only acknowledge those with status? Are you only concerned about those you think can do you some good? It's been said that the way to tell great leaders is to watch the way they treat little people.

Love Them Anyway

Throughout your life you will encounter people who betray you, talk behind your back, break promises, steal from you, envy you, belittle you, or turn their backs on your friendship. Love them anyway. This is probably one of the most difficult things to do. Most of us find it impossible.

It's easy to be nice to friends and people who treat us well. That's not much of a challenge. But to extend kindness to people who treat us badly takes remarkable spirit. Lincoln was vilified in the newspapers and by politicians who despised him. He was called an ape, sub-human, and worse. How did he respond? With self-deprecating humor, patience, and forbearance. He did not allow his enemies to bring him down to their level. Jesus Christ was totally innocent. But he was whipped, beaten, spat upon, and executed in the cruelest of ways. Yet, with his dying breath, he prayed that his enemies be forgiven.

How do you treat those who wish to hurt you? Do you have the strength of character to avoid descending to their level? Can you love them anyway?

Don't Expect the Scales to Balance

There is one simple truth that we have to come to grips with: *Life isn't fair*. If we expect the scales to balance, we're only going to be disappointed. Bad things *do* happen to good people.

So what should we do about it? Simply, do what is right and things will usually work out for the best.

Sure, you'll have setbacks and encounter people who don't play by the rules. But you'll sleep well at night with a clear conscience.

Rest assured, in the final judgment at the end of our lives, the Ultimate Judge will weigh what we've done and *the scales will balance*. "Blessed are they who hunger and thirst for justice, for they shall have their fill."

Do you waste precious time and energy complaining that life isn't fair? Look around. There are many people in this world who have been dealt a tougher hand than you have. Every day, they cope with far more misery, hardship, and injustice than you ever will. Remember the old saying, "I once complained that I had no shoes, but then I met a man who had no feet."

"Evil Triumphs When Good Men Do Nothing"

Neville Chamberlain signed the Munich Pact in September 1938, negotiating with Hitler to settle the question of Czechoslovakia. The agreement signed by Britain, France, Italy, and Germany gave the Sudetenland, a resource rich area of Czechoslovakia, (one-fifth of the country on the German speaking border) to Germany with other areas going to Hungary and Poland.

Returning in triumph to Britain at Heston Airport on September 30, Chamberlain told a cheering crowd, "I believe it is peace in our time."

The peace did not last long. Germany took the rest of Czechoslovakia six months after the agreement was signed. Less than a year later, the world was once again at war. Appeasement in the face of evil never works. It merely promotes greater evil.

Do you have the courage to confront evil? Or does your passive attitude allow it to grow? Do you remain silent to avoid making waves? As a leader, do people know what principles you stand for?

Don't Let Evil Discourage You

It's hard not to become discouraged when we open the paper every morning and read about the evil all around us. Rapes, bombings, genocide, child molestation, sniper attacks, murders, and mayhem fill the pages. All of us have had the thought, "What is this world coming to!"

But perhaps we can take comfort in this fact: *The reason it's news is that it's the exception.* The vast majority of people in the world are good, and every day they are making positive contributions in their own little corners of the world. In fact, their basic goodness is so commonplace, it isn't *newsworthy*.

So don't let evil discourage you. Spread your own light every day and resolve to make the world a better place. The collective contributions of the good people in this world far outweigh the bad.

Have you allowed yourself to be overwhelmed,

disheartened, and immobilized by the evil around you? Have you overlooked the good that actually exists and your own ability to contribute to a better world? Realize that good is destined to one day triumph over evil, and you have a large part to play in that ultimate victory. Let that empower your leadership in a troubled world.

Don't Take It Personally

There's no question that words can be damaging and hurtful—*if we let them*! But in the book, *The Four Agreements*, we are reminded, "Don't take it personally."

Often, the harmful things people say reveal far more about *themselves* than they do about *us*. They are usually projecting their own shortcomings or feelings of inadequacy.

The best response to criticism is to be brutally honest with yourself. Evaluate it for elements of truth. Are several people saying the same thing? Is there a consistent theme? If so, work on a plan for self-improvement. Use their comments to become a better person.

But unfair or unjust criticism is entirely different. Never allow it to damage your self-esteem. It really tells you more about the critic than it does yourself.

Do you evaluate criticism honestly for potential self-improvement? Are you able to ignore unjust criticism? Are you careful with your own words?

Do you guard against back biting on your team? Do you air differences on your team in a constructive way?

Take a Stand

You're either a spectator in life, or a player. You either live by your principles, or abandon them. There is no middle ground.

"Evil triumphs when good men do nothing." *Pity the man or woman who has nothing they're willing to die for.* Is that even a life worth living?

How about you, do you stand up for what you believe in, or easily surrender to adversity?

Make a Difference

People often ask, what difference can just one person make? What's the use of even trying? But John F. Kennedy won the 1960 presidential election by an average of one vote per precinct across the nation. President Andrew Johnson, Lincoln's successor, was impeached, but stayed in office because of one vote.

Loren Eiseley, in his book of essays, *The Star Throwers*, tells an interesting story. A young man on the beach observes an older man stooping down, picking something up, and throwing it as far as he could back into the ocean. He did this over and over. As the young man got closer, he could see that the older man was picking up starfish.

He asked him, "Hey, there are thousands of starfish along this beach, as far as the eye can see. Just what are you doing?" "Well," the man replied, "these starfish were left stranded at high tide, and I'm saving them by throwing them back in the ocean." "Are you crazy?" the young man asked. "You'll never make a difference with the thousands out here." The older man just ignored the question, reached down, and flung another one into the sea saying, "Made a difference to that one, didn't I?"

Where would we be without Abraham Lincoln, George Washington, Rosa Parks, Martin Luther King, Jr., and hundreds more? Do you still doubt that one person can make a difference?

Understand the Power of Forgiveness

We often look at forgiveness—which, in itself, is hard enough—as something we do *for other people*.

But if you examine it more closely, forgiveness is also something we do for *ourselves*. Remembering slights, holding grudges, and seeking revenge is like acid, eating away its container. If we hold anger inside, it damages *us*. And the *longer* we hold on to it, the more damage it does, physically, mentally, and spiritually.

Forgiveness is liberating, both asking for it and granting it. When we ask others to forgive us, it allows us to let go of the guilt for past transgressions. This holds true, *whether they choose to forgive us or not*. When we forgive others, it doesn't mean that we've forgotten what they did, just that we're not going to let it poison us anymore.

The Lord's Prayer says, "Forgive us our trespasses, as we forgive those who trespass against us." A frightening double-edged sword, isn't it? It asks us to examine our own ability to forgive others, because that's the standard which will be applied to us. George Herbert tells us, "He who cannot forgive breaks the bridge over which he himself must cross."

How well are you able to ask for and grant forgiveness? Are you aware of the damaging effects of holding grudges and harboring thoughts of revenge? Viewed in that light, does hurting yourself even make sense?

Forget About It

"Real Age," a guide to good health and longevity, tells us not to keep rehashing old worries. It could harm your health.

A recent study revealed that recalling a past trauma or emotional event may cause an emotionally driven increase in blood pressure that is just as intense as the spike that occurred during the original event. Over time, chronic spikes in blood pressure could place undue stress on your heart.

Do you hold grudges or keep rehashing unpleasant events? Are you aware of the negative effects on your health? If so, let go of them. They are poisonous.

Nothing Happens in a Vacuum

Sometimes we make the mistake of thinking we exist in isolation, that the things we do have no effect on anyone else. But nothing happens in a vacuum.

Everything that we do, good or bad, will be felt in some way, *eventually*. There are no victimless crimes. At the very least, evil will affect the doer, even if it seemingly harms no one else. And by affecting the doer, it diminishes us all, for each of us is a part of humanity.

Do you believe that every action has an effect? If so, are you a force for good?

Recognize the Unsung Heroes

Often we become star struck, placing too much value on celebrity. Worshiping the rich and famous has become a national obsession. With cult-like fervor, we hang on their every word, giving them far too much importance. Sadly, movie stars or famous athletes are able to carry large blocks of voters simply because of their celebrity, not their ideas. But a closer examination often shows that they lack any depth of character at all. In fact, their pampered lives have only turned them into prima donnas who really haven't accomplished much in life, other than being famous.

We might learn more wisdom from the single mom working two jobs while trying to raise four kids.

Or the tired coal miner, coming home from a hard day's work, but still willing to toss a baseball with his son in the back yard. Or the underpaid school teacher, working late grading papers and preparing the next day's lesson plan.

Perhaps the terrorist attack on the World Trade Center taught us who our real heroes are. They're the everyday men and women earning paychecks, raising families, and caring for aging parents. They've gained true wisdom by living lives that are *real and meaningful*.

I doubt if anyone can name the last five Miss America winners. How about the last five MVP's of the National Football League? Or the last five Olympic gold medalists in the 100-meter dash? *But we can all remember five coaches or teachers who had real impact on our lives.* These are the unsung heroes who really matter! And these are the people we should really be listening to.

Whom do you listen to on your team? Do you ever pay attention to the little guy, or only those with power, an impressive title, and a fancy office? Do you dismiss a good idea, simply because the person offering it has little status? If so, you're missing out on some of the best input. However, if you show a willingness to listen to *everyone's* ideas, regardless of their rank in the company, you'll receive so many good ones it will be hard to implement them all. Word will soon get out, "The boss really cares what we think."

Acknowledge Your Benefactors

No one ever makes it on her own. While we might like to think our achievements are solo efforts, there were a lot of people who helped along the way. Often they were the unsung heroes of your past: parents, teachers, friends, coaches, and other teammates.

If you take all the credit yourself, it is highly unlikely that you'll ever get help again. That's when you'll discover that you really didn't make it on your own. But by then, it may be impossible to assemble a new team. No one will want to worship at your altar again.

Are you a solo act? Or do you acknowledge the people that helped you along the way?

Be Ready to Throw a Life Ring

Naval vessels always have a lookout posted on the "fantail," the stern of the ship. His most important job is to be alert for a man overboard, and throw him a life ring. The vigilance of that lookout means life or death for a man falling in the water. In most cases, it's his last chance to be saved.

There are times when we are like that lookout. We could be a friend's last chance for survival. He may be without hope, overcome by personal problems, addictions, or even contemplating suicide. If we're watchful, we'll recognize his call for help.

But recognizing it is only the first step. *Now we*

must be willing to throw the life ring. This may be as simple as a kind or encouraging word, advising them to seek professional help, giving them financial assistance, or just showing a willingness to listen. Never underestimate the impact you can have. It can make all the difference in the world to someone in need of rescue. It may even save his life.

Are you a good lookout? Are you overlooking signals that a friend is in trouble? What is your intuition telling you about a potential problem? More importantly, are you ready to throw a life ring?

Seek Respect, Not Popularity

Some people make the mistake of seeking popularity, thinking it will lead to respect. Usually they end up with neither.

It is better to stand up for your principles, not caring what people think. Trying to curry favor and be all things to all people will only frustrate you. People will see you as someone who leads by opinion polls—and not worthy of respect.

True friendships and inspiring leadership can only be built on a foundation of respect. Nothing else works.

Are you overly concerned with what people think? Are you swayed by public opinion, or steadfast? Is your leadership based on a bedrock of guiding principles, or do you change like shifting winds? Is popularity more important to you than respect?

Use the Power of Words

Never underestimate the power of words. Whoever said, "The pen is mightier than the sword," understood this. Words can be used for great good or egregious evil.

Hitler used words to convince an entire nation that they were a pure, Aryan race, even though the concept of *racial purity* is preposterous to begin with. Blinded by Hitler's lies, his people helped him carry out his diabolical plan of genocide. European Jews, gypsies, and other minorities were condemned, simply because they *were unworthy to be called pure Germans*. Over six million innocent men, women, and children were murdered in holocaust gas chambers!

In the darkest days of the Civil War, when our very survival was in doubt, Abraham Lincoln's words stirred the conscience of a nation. His simple, yet eloquent, condemnation of slavery appealed to the innate decency of the American people. His words rallied the country and kept England out of the war. Today, many of Lincoln's speeches are regarded as some of the most powerful words ever spoken.

Be mindful of your words. Choose them wisely. They can do great harm or tremendous good. And remember, like an arrow loosed, they are impossible to bring back.

Are you careful with words? Do you use them for good and helping others?

Never Underestimate the Power of a Kind Word

Everyone needs acknowledgement, to know they matter. An encouraging word has unbelievable power to motivate. But it must be *absolutely sincere*. Anything less undermines your credibility and does nothing for the person hearing it, except perhaps, to sow doubt in their own abilities, "Why am I receiving false praise?"

As a leader, open your eyes and manage by walking around. There's a lot of good happening around you. *Your job is to notice it and acknowledge it!* You'll never come close to seeing it all. But don't miss seeing as much as you can. That well-timed word of praise is energizing to your team and gives a remarkable boost to morale. They'll know you really care about them. And give acknowledgement as soon as you see it. It means far more than some award given long after the fact.

Are you aware of how much good is going on behind the scenes? Do you make an effort to acknowledge it? Are you stuck behind your desk? Do people on your team see you walking around every day, interested in them? Do you ask about their families in addition to their work? Or are all of your conversations with them merely superficial, lacking genuine interest?

Teach and Share Knowledge

We really don't know something thoroughly until we can teach it to others. It is the hidden key to mastery. But sometimes we selfishly hoard knowledge because we fear we're giving up our edge on the competition, or the thing that makes us special.

But teaching and sharing knowledge actually benefit both mentor and student. By having to articulate what we know, we learn it better ourselves. And our student now has knowledge that he can one day pass on to others. The Bible tells us, "Don't hide your light under a bushel basket." Remember, any knowledge you have was once itself a gift to *you*. Polish it and pass it on. It was meant to be shared.

Are you selfishly hoarding your gifts? Hiding your light? Remember, every one of us is tasked with leaving a legacy, making the world a better place than the one we inherited.

See the Good in People

We often allow the faults of others to be magnified and overlook the good things people really do. This can be especially true of our own family members or friends. We nag our children and spouses, or criticize friends and fellow workers to the point where we begin to believe they can't do anything right. Sadly, *they* also start believing this, and it becomes a self-fulfilling prophecy. They lose heart.

It's better to look for the good in others. Even when the negative actually *does* outweigh the positive, *try to catch them in the act of doing something right, then build on it*. Over time, you'll boost their self-esteem and they will seek to live up to the high opinion you have of them. Negative comments only tear them down.

Do you view people through a negative filter? How do you think that affects them? What steps can you take to view them in a different light? What are some positives you can see in their behavior that you can build on, *right now*?

Demonstrating through your actions that you're in their corner sends a powerful message. Most people will respond to that kind of positive reinforcement in a dramatic way. Be patient; you'll soon begin to see the effects.

Remember, You Can't Do It Alone

Earlier we talked about John Donne, who said it best, "No man is an island." While we may cling to the romanticized American folklore of the rugged individual, making it on his own, that's seldom the way it works in real life.

Sooner or later we realize that we can't do it all by ourselves. Henry Ford introduced the idea of the assembly line. But it would have gone nowhere without workers to make it happen. Even athletes who play individual sports like golf and tennis have their coaches, nutritionists, and sports psychologists.

All of mankind's greatest achievements were team efforts. When we look more closely, even solo accomplishments most certainly had the early encouragement of parents, coaches, and family members. Only when we work together in concert do we reach our full potential as human beings.

Are you a solo act? Are you so arrogant that you believe you did it without any assistance? If so, then you need to examine more closely all the ways people helped you along the way.

III

Optimum Team Leadership

Promote and Value Teamwork

Everything we do, good or bad, eventually rises to the surface. While we may think it will never be felt, just the opposite is true. The old school yard game, tug of war, illustrates this.

Ten people are at each end of a long rope. One member on one of the teams is a little tired that day and not really giving his best effort. He's thinking, "I'm really not into this today. Besides, with nine other people on the rope, who's going to know the difference whether I'm really pulling hard or not?"

He's right. It would be very hard to pinpoint someone who was slacking off, except for one thing: *The flag in the middle of the rope is going in the other team's direction.* They're winning. That's the point: every action, positive or negative, will eventually be felt in some way on your team. The truth—and that honest effort—always comes out.

Having a team of all stars doesn't guarantee success either. We've all witnessed a group of selfish individuals, every one of them extremely talented, fail miserably. However, winning teams are composed of unselfish members who always give their best effort and subordinate their own egos for the good of the team.

As a leader, are you willing to play a supporting role when that's what the team needs most? Do you empower others in order to develop them for increased leadership responsibilities? Do you lead by example, always giving your best effort?

Create Winning Teams

Mickey Mantle, the great Hall of Fame center fielder for the New York Yankees, used to say that he could identify a winning team, even if he was unfamiliar with the sport, simply by observing the players' behavior in the locker room after a game. In a losing locker room, he saw lots of sniping among the players, lots of blame being spread around. Or maybe the locker room was as quiet as a tomb. On the other hand, in a winning locker room, Mickey would observe just the opposite: lots of back slapping, praise, appreciation for each other, and laughter.

Lou Holtz, the great head football coach at Notre Dame for many years, assembled his players before the first spring practice of 1988. At that meeting, he asked the players to make a pact: *They would never say anything negative about a teammate the entire year*. Those players kept that promise to each other, and Notre Dame won the national championship.

How are things in your organization? Do snipers roam freely? Is there a lot of back biting, jealousy? Or do people go that extra mile to help each other out? Is there camaraderie, laughter, friendship? Would Mickey Mantle describe your "locker room" as a winning one? If not, what are you doing as a leader to change things?

Be a Servant Leader

The idea of servant leadership goes back 2,000 years. "The last shall be first, and the first last." Leaders must put juniors first.

Often however, as we climb the corporate ladder, just the opposite happens. We get caught up in our own self-importance and begin to enjoy the perks of seniority. Worse yet, we come to *expect* them. Somehow we begin to think our own opinions are the only ones that matter since, obviously, we're the only ones who have achieved "enlightenment." We easily dismiss the viewpoints of those "less gifted" and look to surround ourselves with yes men who will reinforce the exalted opinion we already have of ourselves and our own ideas.

Has arrogance closed you off to the ideas of others, especially those junior to you? Do subordinates always feel your heavy hand on the tiller and never get to steer for themselves? Would your team ever think of you as a servant leader, someone who puts them first?

Understand the Value of Incentives

If we accept the premise that every person is unique, then it follows that we are all motivated in different ways. Yet we continue to try to provide incentives in a "one size fits all" fashion.

While monetary rewards may be perfect for some, others would prefer public recognition and acknowledgement. Then there are those who are naturally shy, and being put in the spotlight is their worst nightmare. Instead, a private and personal "well done" from the boss makes their day. Often, people on your team will appreciate a combination of several incentives.

The possibilities are endless and only limited by your imagination: time off, dinner certificate, bonus check, certificate of appreciation, parking space, family pass to Disneyland, camping equipment, gym membership, mountain bike, movie tickets—or a new Corvette.

How will you know what incentives matter most? Here is where the value of a personal, one-on-one interview pays great dividends: *Ask them*. They may give you ideas you never even thought of. Good leaders really know their people. In fact, there's nothing more important.

Once your team understands that you are genuinely interested in them as *people* and not just workers, you begin to unleash their unlimited potential. They will reward you with their loyalty and you will become a powerful leader.

As a leader, what incentives do you use to motivate your team? Have you ever asked them their preferences? Have you done one-on-one interviews to really get to know each person? What do you know about their families, hobbies, interests, and goals? Or do you limit your interest only to their function at work?

Set the Example

Leadership is 100% example, period! Everything we learn about leadership comes from watching leaders in action. In fact, we really don't care much about what leaders *say*, especially if their words don't match their actions.

Think back. We get our first cues from our parents. Like dry sponges, we soak up everything: their mannerisms, speech patterns, behavior, how they discipline, and so forth. The same is true of our own leadership style. It becomes a composite of what we learned by watching others. (We also learn from bad leadership as well as good, hopefully deciding never to treat other people the way that poor leaders once treated us.)

As a leader, do you set the example and lead by your actions? Or are you more concerned with your position and privileges than the welfare of your people? Do you pitch in when they need help, or are you a prima donna? There should be no job beneath your dignity.

Value and Promote Friendship

In 1942, U.S. Marines on Guadalcanal were engaged in some of the most horrific fighting of the war: vicious hand to hand combat, suicidal banzai charges, malaria, and limited supplies of food and ammunition. They weren't even expected to survive.

Somehow, for some inexplicable reason, the Marines were able to hang on and win the battle of Guadalcanal. No one could figure out why until they asked the individual Marines. Here is what each of them said: "I didn't want to let my buddy down in the next fox hole. If he was willing to fight on, so was I."

Is the value of friendship overlooked on your team? Are workers expected to work at peak efficiency all day with set times and limits for coffee breaks and lunch? Is all activity about billable hours only, or do you leave room for true friendships to develop?

Believe in Your Intuition

Intuition is called the sixth sense. If you've ever said to yourself, "I *knew* that was going to happen!" then you've experienced intuition. Many inputs are constantly being processed by the mind—itself a marvelous and mysterious tool—at the subconscious level.

For example, without even being aware of it, we are continuously making judgments about what other drivers are going to do on the freeway. Maybe it's the way they look in their side view mirrors before they change lanes, or their inattention while using a cell phone, or an overall sense of their aggressive driving habits. We process hundreds of these cues from the drivers all around us in milliseconds, without conscious thought. We become mentally prepared for the unexpected, actually "knowing" it was going to happen beforehand because of this marvelous gift called intuition.

Just as we use intuition while driving, we can use it in leadership. People are constantly giving us cues about their feelings and motivations. We need to observe such things as body language, inflection, tone of voice, and mood. If we really *listen* to what they are telling us, *at the subconscious level*, we can solve many problems before they catch us by surprise.

As a leader, do you listen to your intuition? Or do you ignore it simply because it defies rational explanation? Did you hire the wrong people because you failed to follow your gut feel when you first interviewed them? Did you ever make a poor decision, kicking yourself later because you sensed it was a mistake from the very beginning? These are all examples of failing to follow your intuition.

Don't make that mistake. Harness intuition's power. Trust your gut.

Listen!

Public speaking courses abound, but how many of us have ever been to a *listening course*? There are very few. And yet, a good conversation requires both: a speaker and a listener who's paying attention.

Isn't it interesting that we were given two ears,

but one mouth? Maybe that should tell us something about the importance of listening versus speaking. But too often our conversations are *dueling monologues*. We don't even bother to listen as we wait for our own turn to speak.

Dr. Stephen Covey tells us, "Seek to understand, before being understood." Good advice. *Listening adds to our store of knowledge; speaking does not*. Listening also sends a powerful message to the person speaking: "I have respect for you and what you are saying." If we set that example with our own empathetic listening, there's a good chance it will be reciprocated.

How well do you listen? Do you monopolize the conversation because you're the boss? Do you think you're the only one with good ideas? Are you missing good inputs because of your attitude?

As a leader, be the last to speak. That will prevent your opinion from biasing the discussion. More untainted views will be voiced that way. People are more likely to say what's on their minds rather than what they think the boss wants to hear. Give praise to anyone willing to offer a contrary opinion. They are showing courage and may be saying the exact thing that needs to be heard. Yes men are of no value.

Communicate!

On any team, when a problem occurs, you can invariably track it down to poor communication. You will *always* have communication. Human beings can't stand not knowing and will make something up if they have to. Whenever good communication is lacking, assumptions and rumors will fill the void.

When Lee Iacocca was trying to save Chrysler from bankruptcy in the 1980s, he opened up the books to all employees. His communication to them was clear, forthright, and direct. He made them understand their financial situation was desperate, "I have lots of jobs at $18.75, but *none* at $25.00." If the union workers didn't agree to wage concessions, Chrysler would not survive. Everyone needed to understand they were all in this together. It's amazing how hard people will work to bail out the lifeboat, *if that's the only lifeboat*.

Do you always have open and honest communications using every available means of getting the word out? Do you ever hoard information as a way of retaining power and control? Do you open up the books and show employees the company's "bottom line"? Are you afraid to open yourself up to the *tough questions*?

Let Go

We often cling to things because "Well, that's the way we've always done it." There's something comfortable about the familiar. We all have our security blankets.

But sometimes they get in the way of real breakthroughs. I suppose, a baby in the womb, if she were able to choose, would stay in that warm, nurturing environment forever. But then she would never experience the beauty and light of the outside world. Past success can often be our tightest pair of handcuffs, trapping us in the present reality and preventing us from looking for even better ways of doing things.

Years ago, it was once suggested that we should close the U. S. Patent Office because everything had already been invented and nothing new was possible. It's amazing to think that people really thought that way, but they did.

Through the years, we marveled at the LP record, then the 8-track tape, and later the compact disc. Soon we'll be able to download a century's worth of music on a single computer chip. And who knows what lies beyond that? Perhaps holograms where the former Beatles actually give a concert in your own living room? Climbing one peak just gives us a better view of the next one.

Bold leaders dare to dream of visions beyond our present reach. In 1961, John F. Kennedy challenged the nation to put a man on the moon before that decade ended. Henry Ford told his engineers to design a V-8 engine, even though they thought it was impossible at the time. But Ford simply refused to listen to doubters and locked them all in a room until they came up with the very design he knew was possible.

As a leader, what are you hanging onto that has outlived its usefulness? Was your company once known as the greatest manufacturer of buggy whips?

Would you rather have a *competitor* discover the next breakthrough? Then why isn't your team working on it right now? Is there any reason to believe we've reached the high water mark of human achievement, especially when we look back at our history?

Use Stories and Analogies to Communicate

Our greatest communicators were *storytellers*. Abraham Lincoln was known as "the great yarn spinner." As he traveled from town to town, riding the law circuit, people would flock to the local taverns just to hear him tell his amusing, often hilarious stories. In the courtroom, Lincoln would often make his point, to great effect, with an analogy or story.

The Bible is filled with Jesus' parables, stories which illustrate important lessons. And we all grew up hearing *Aesop's Fables*.

Never overlook this powerful way of communicating. It can put an idea into language people immediately understand. People relate to stories.

Do you use stories and analogies to communicate? Are you missing out on this powerful communication tool?

Recognize Leadership at All Levels

An enduring strength of our military is the belief that even the most junior person has the ability to lead. One of the best examples of our confidence in that idea occurred on the beaches of Normandy, June 6, 1944. As landing craft approached Omaha Beach on D-Day, the embarked infantry could hear machine gun bullets ricocheting off the bow ramp. The men inside knew that once the ramp came down, their armored shield would be gone.

As they stormed ashore, the platoon's second lieutenant often made it only fifty yards before he was cut down. The first sergeant might have gone a few more steps before suffering the same fate. So what enabled the platoon to stay together and keep advancing when they lost their leaders? One simple reason: *New leaders took over.* The next senior man willingly took charge.

You'll never know where your junior leaders are hiding if you don't give them a chance to lead. Most of us are familiar with the story of David and Goliath. Who would have thought that a young shepherd boy could slay an invincible giant and later become the king of a great nation? Fortunately, King Saul believed in young David and gave him the chance to prove himself.

How about you? Do you develop potential leaders, or are you afraid of losing power? Do you feel that you have to make every decision, or can you delegate responsibility and give others a chance to lead, make mistakes, and grow?

Beware the Abuse of Power

Power can be very dangerous. Handling it is a challenge for it can quickly go to your head. You get accustomed to preferential treatment and junior workers treating you with deference. Soon you begin to *expect* it. You start thinking of yourself as someone special. You forget what it means to be a servant leader.

You guard your lofty position against all challenges. As the most capable, intelligent, and talented member of the organization, *you* make all the decisions. You behave like George Armstrong Custer—whose hubris led to the massacre of his 7th Cavalry at the Battle of the Little Big Horn in 1876. Once your mind is made up, no one ever overrules a "Custer decision." The boss can never be wrong, or if he is, certainly never admits it.

Is your leadership like George Armstrong Custer's? Do you hoard power? Do you ever admit mistakes? Do you try to cover them up? Are you a solo act? Or do you believe that power shared is power multiplied?

Calm Seas Do Not Make Good Sailors

One of the best ways to have a perfect safety record in aviation is to park all the aircraft in the hangar and never fly. Sailors do not become good mariners by staying tied up at the pier and never venturing out beyond the shelter of the harbor.

Playing it safe is fine—if you want your skills to atrophy! But greatness comes through risk and challenge, or as Teddy Roosevelt said, "by being in the arena." He went on to say, "It is better to fail in a courageous attempt than to count yourself among those timid souls who know neither victory nor defeat."

Are you playing it safe on the sidelines? Are you a spectator in the game of life? Have you infected your team with that attitude? There's a time-honored saying, "He who will not risk, cannot win." How closely do you follow it?

Take Note of Your Surroundings, Then Act

Pause, observe, and reflect. Don't let chaos confuse you. Rather, be the eye of the hurricane, calm, centered. Allow your senses to take in all inputs, then engage your best ally, intuition. What is it telling you? What's your gut feel?

Once you've gained a sense of what's really going on, take action. Do what your intuition dictates. Now! Don't be a deer in the headlights. Don't fear making mistakes. Rather, fear inaction. History favors the bold.

Do you follow your instincts when faced with chaos? Do you take bold action? Have you infused that attitude in your team, or do they live in fear of making the slightest misstep? Remember, fear is normal. What you do in spite of your fear is what counts.

Pay Attention to Details

"It's the little things that count." Having spent a good part of my life in naval aviation, I've seen cases where a single missing cotter key in a flight control caused the deaths of eight crewmen. Think how you would have felt if you had been the mechanic who forgot to replace it.

Vince Lombardi, the great coach of the Green Bay Packers, would run the same play in practice over and over again until it was executed to perfection. He probably drove his Packers crazy with his painstaking preparation. But come game time on Sunday, even though the opposing team may have known Jimmy Taylor, the Packers' running back, was going to come sweeping around the end led by blocking linemen Forrest Gregg and Jerry Kramer, they couldn't stop the play. It was just too well executed.

Everyone thinks that top performers are a

quantum leap better than everybody else. But Picabo Street won the Olympic downhill by a mere $1/100^{th}$ of a second. In reality, they only have a slight competitive edge. And usually that edge is attention to detail. After open heart surgery, don't you hope that your surgeon is counting the sponges?

Does your team have the attention to detail that leads to excellence?

Sports Can Teach Life Lessons

Sports can teach us a lot about life. Hustle, hard work, self-sacrifice, and teamwork win games. But teams composed of all stars, even with enormous *individual talent*, often fail because they don't work together. Each star is more concerned about his individual stats than how the *team* performs.

The adage, "It's never over until the final whistle," has another valuable lesson. Give up, and you'll never experience the thrill of a comeback victory.

Rest on your laurels, and you probably won't repeat as champions. Show good sportsmanship. Be humble in victory and gracious in defeat. Always play fair. Never run up the score on an opponent; it may come back to haunt you. Learn as much from your defeats as your victories. All of these sayings from the world of sports have much to teach us.

What lessons do you see from sports that can be applied to life, to your team? Emulating a championship sports team is a great way to run a company.

Swing for the Fences

One of the most decorated fighting units of World War II was the 100th Battalion of the 442 Infantry Regiment, composed entirely of Nisei soldiers, second generation Japanese-Americans.

These were amazing fighting men. Even though many of their family members were being held in Japanese internment camps back in the United States, they fought valiantly for their country against the Germans in Europe. Their bravery was so renowned that they were also known as "The Purple Heart Battalion."

"Go for broke" was the 442's motto because these legendary soldiers gave every last measure of themselves in battle. They were tenacious and unstoppable.

Babe Ruth was one of the greatest home run hitters in baseball history. To see him swing at a pitch gave true meaning to the words, "Swing for the fences." Babe held nothing back. While hitting all those home runs, he also led the league in strikeouts, but that never discouraged him. He wasn't afraid of failure. He was never tentative at the plate. He knew that failure goes hand in hand with great achievement. Just as the 442 knew that victory often meant the ultimate sacrifice.

Are you willing to swing for the fences? Can you commit to your vision and put it all on the line, holding nothing back? Remember, half-hearted efforts usually result in failure.

Just Shoot the Ball

Robert Horry of the Los Angeles Lakers had an uncanny ability to sink game-winning shots at the final buzzer. After another one of his last second baskets gave his team the victory, he was asked by reporters, "What do you *think about* when you get the ball in those critical situations?" Robert replied, "I can't *think*; if I did, I'd miss. I just have to react and let my body take over."

We've all heard of "paralysis through analysis." It's just what Robert was talking about. You need to *get your mind out of the way* and let your body take over. Sometimes we refer to this as "being in the zone." Do you think Pete Sampras thinks about how high to toss the tennis ball when he serves? Of course not! He just throws it up and hits it.

Granted, it takes years of training to create that kind of automatic response, or muscle memory. But often, after we've reached that level of training, we start second guessing ourselves. Our minds allow self-doubt to creep in instead of just allowing all that training to flow naturally, *unencumbered by thinking*.

Did you ever notice how basketball teams sometimes shoot very poorly in the opening minutes of a championship game? The reason: *They're thinking too much and worrying about making mistakes instead of just going out and enjoying the competitive challenge*.

How about you? Are you able to let go and let

your training take over? Or are you allowing your mind's negative self talk to take you out of the zone? When you make a mistake, are you able to leave it in the past where it belongs, or do you let it hinder your performance in the present?

Get up off the Mat and Never Give Up

Failure doesn't matter. We all fail because we're all human. More important is what we do after being thrown to the mat. That shows our true character.

The Chrysler Corporation was ready to go out of business and declare bankruptcy in the 1980s. But Lee Iacocca, the new president, led the company back from the brink of disaster by convincing his team to keep trying and not give up. They re-dedicated themselves to building quality automobiles at affordable prices. All employees agreed to wage concessions, and Lee Iacocca himself took a $1.00 annual salary. He would receive other incentives only if the company succeeded. Chrysler defied the odds and made a complete recovery.

On October 29, 1941, Winston Churchill came to the Harrow School in England to give the commencement address. The crowd awaited his eloquent words with great anticipation. Finally, he rose to his feet, stepped up to the microphone and said, "Never give up; never give up; never give up." Then he sat down.

Those words summed up his whole approach to life. The game is not over until the final whistle blows. It may sound trite, but think of the wisdom in that idea. The British were swept off the beaches of Dunkirk, totally defeated. But their retreat wasn't the end. They regrouped to fight on in Africa, Sicily, and finally Europe, pushing the Nazis all the way back to Berlin. The British endured the worst Hitler had to throw at them and came out victorious because they simply refused to give up.

One of the greatest experiences in all of sports, or life for that matter, is the come-from-behind victory. Nothing is sweeter than defying the odds and winning when all hope is seemingly gone. But you will *never* experience that unbelievable exhilaration if you quit.

What about your team? How do they handle seeming defeat? Do you teach them perseverance and tenacity? Are they willing to defy the odds and prove the experts wrong? As a leader, do you display a fighting spirit that permeates your entire team? Are they willing to fight on, no matter what? Has your team ever savored the come-from-behind victory? Remember, nothing is sweeter than the triumph over the impossible.

Hustle Cures Anxiety

Sometimes before a championship game, athletes feel tight. Their nerves are on edge and they feel anxious, which prevents them from playing their best.

In basketball, for example, this tightness results in shots clanging off the rim—those infamous "bricks." Even star players are off their game.

One of the best cures for this anxiety is hustle. Play your toughest defense, contest every rebound, scramble for loose balls. This siphons off excess nervous energy and provides an antidote for game day jitters. Soon confidence grows and you get into the zone. You stop worrying about making mistakes and are able to play up to your potential.

This works in other challenging situations as well. Get moving. Do something. Take action. Fear and anxiety will no longer paralyze you if you start hustling.

Do you let anxiety or fear of failure paralyze you? Do you become the proverbial deer in the headlights? If so, get moving. Hustle will reduce tension.

Keep Your Eye on the Ball

Our greatest athletes have a remarkable ability to focus on the task at hand and block everything else out. Many claim to not even hear the fans when they are on the mound pitching in the World Series, shooting a basketball at Madison Square Garden, or hitting a golf ball on the 18th tee at the Masters.

Martial arts teach us to concentrate on one attacker at a time. Otherwise we lose focus and our efforts become scattered and ineffective. Like the sands passing through the hourglass, we can only deal with one grain at a time.

What's your focus? Do you concentrate on doing one thing well? Or do you juggle several things, doing them all poorly? Recent scientific studies tell us that multi-tasking leads to substandard performance. Not only that, the resulting higher levels of stress have serious health consequences as well. Are you pulling members of your team in several different directions at once? Do they know what your most important goal is? Do you let them focus on it? Or is your impatience and meddling a major distraction?

Give It Your Best Shot

Always do your best and you'll never have any regrets. Nothing is more haunting than to look back at a missed opportunity and know in your heart you really didn't give it your best, especially when it turns out that a little more effort might have made all the difference in the world.

Picabo Street won the women's Olympic downhill by $1/100^{th}$ of a second. She went all out, knowing an opportunity like that might only come along once in a lifetime. She had no idea that the margin of victory would be so slim, but left nothing to chance. Think how she would have felt if she had let up anywhere along the course during her gold medal run.

If we're honest with ourselves, we can all look back and see those missed opportunities that were due to a lack of commitment or effort. Rather than mourn them obsessively—which is a waste of time anyway—resolve to never put yourself in that position again. From now on, resolve to do your best and you'll never have any regrets.

Can you remember a time when you gave a half-hearted effort? When you let your team down? How did you feel afterward? Was there a hollow feeling in the pit of your stomach, a sense of missed opportunity? Doing your best gives you immunity from those feelings. You'll draw comfort from the fact that, win or lose, you gave it your best effort.

Recognize Blind Alleys

Sometimes, despite our best efforts, plans go wrong. We find ourselves in a blind alley. What began as a promising opportunity, becomes a dry well, a dead end.

Yet we stubbornly continue to spin our wheels in the mud, rather than admit we made a mistake. But this just makes things worse. It's better to say, "Hey, we goofed," and start work on extricating yourselves.

History shows us that *first attempts* are seldom rewarded. Rather, the old adage, "Success is the last event in a long string of failures," is more often the case. Blind alleys, failures, and even disasters are the norm for courageous teams. They don't fear making mistakes, but make multiple attempts, knowing that a few of those will reap great rewards.

Do you recognize blind alleys? Can you admit mistakes and reverse course? Do bumps in the road make you stop trying? Do you recognize that every failure is actually a marvelous teacher? Learn to treat failure as a necessary step toward great achievement; then setbacks won't bother you.

Find Order in Chaos

"Chaos theory" tells us that there is order in seeming chaos. What may appear random, jumbled, and disorganized actually has patterns and designs, if we just look more closely.

For example, with all the rivers on the planet, you might be surprised to learn that there are only five basic types. And as astronomers look more deeply into the farthest reaches of the universe, they see that the billions of galaxies fall into only a few basic patterns. Wherever you look in nature, there is evidence of a Grand Architect at work. Stars and galaxies continuously collide and are destroyed, but new ones, with symmetry and beauty, are born from that chaos and destruction.

Why should this be important to us? Simply because our own lives, as part of the natural order, follow chaos theory. The destruction or death of things we hold dear is often necessary for new and better patterns to emerge. Out of failed relationships or business deals, new opportunities arise. What may seem like chaos and destruction is actually rebirth. It's Nature's way of evolving and improving. New possibilities are always there if we look for them.

Do you look for new opportunities in what may

seem like chaos? Are you able to see new and better patterns emerging? Are you willing to explore these new possibilities? It's been said that the one constant we have is change, and great leaders are change managers.

Recognize the Value of Mistakes

One of your first objectives as a leader is to develop a healthy attitude about making mistakes. Everyone on your team needs to appreciate that mistakes are essential to growth, learning, and ultimately, success. It's been said that "Success is often the last event in a long line of failures." You must be willing to fail in order to learn. Caution might seem safe, but it is not the source of progress. Take a lesson from the turtle: it only moves forward when it sticks its neck out.

Thomas Edison tried 10,000 different materials for the filament of the electric light, all of them abject failures. When he was asked, "Mr. Edison, you're no better off than when you started. What have you learned?" He replied, "Well, now I know 10,000 things that don't work." That's the right attitude about making mistakes! Edison wasn't worried about risking his personal prestige and reputation by failing. He stuck his neck out.

As a leader, what is your attitude toward mistakes, yours and those of your team? Do you cover up your own errors in order to avoid embarrassment? Do you somehow think *anyone* is fooled by that? Can members of your team make honest mistakes without retribution? And if not, how do you think that will that affect their attitude about ever trying anything risky?

Leaders must show their teams that it's okay to fail. They need to applaud the *valiant attempt*. This will change the whole culture of the organization. People will stop looking over their shoulders and no longer be afraid of making mistakes. Creativity will flourish!

Face Fear with Courage

Karl Wallenda, patriarch of the great German circus family, "The Flying Wallendas," once said, "Being on the tightrope is living; everything else is waiting." About Wallenda, Warren Bennis commented, "Some people think failure is final. Others gain energy and learn from failure."

In 1962, while performing their incredible seven-person pyramid on the high wire in Detroit, two men fell to their deaths, and a third, Karl's son, was paralyzed from the waist down. *The very next night*, the Wallendas were back up on the high wire, in the finest tradition of "The show must go on," performing their pyramid once again.

What is your attitude about failure? Are you able to use failure as a springboard to learning and future success, or do you let it haunt you? Are you so worried about making mistakes that you no longer take the risks necessary for great achievement? Does this fear paralyze your team?

Burn Your Ships

Shortly after he landed in Mexico, Cortez ordered his ships burned. This sent a powerful message to his followers. Turning back wasn't an option. There was no retreat.

Young boys, faced with a high wall, will often throw their hats to the other side, forcing them to figure out a way to climb over it.

What's *your* level of commitment? Are you more interested in finding excuses—reasons why it *can't* be done—or solving the problem? The solution may not be evident, but if you *believe* it exists, your team will find it. As a leader, give them a vision; then get out of their way.

Don't Fear the Great Leap

Sometimes a new idea is so extraordinary that it shakes the very foundation of what went before.

Gunpowder made once impregnable castle walls obsolete. Farming, and the rise of cities, displaced hunter gathering. Freedom and democracy unleashed human potential in unimagined ways over despotism. The sun being accepted as the center of the solar system allowed astronomy to make sense. Microscopic organisms being discovered as the cause of many diseases allowed great advances in medicine.

We often cling to old ideas simply because we're comfortable with them, whether they make sense or not. But sometimes, the only thing required for a great leap forward is an open and curious mind and a willingness to challenge old assumptions. That often requires courage to overcome ridicule—or even death itself. But those having that kind of fortitude have often made some of the greatest contributions to mankind.

Are you able to break with the past and take the great leap forward? What are you clinging to that doesn't really work or make sense anymore? As a leader, can you embrace change? Are you willing to think in new ways? Are you listening to what the devil's advocates are saying, or ignoring them because it's not what you want to hear?

Let Failure Empower You

Sometimes it takes a two-by-four on the side of the head to wake us up. When we fail miserably, we realize the need to change. We finally admit that we've wandered into a blind alley and are going nowhere.

This awakening should be a call to action. Rather than being stunned by failure, get back on your feet and do something. Ask other members of your team to help you evaluate the situation. This is no time for yes men. Make an honest self-appraisal of what went wrong, then fix it.

You may be surprised to discover that failure was just what was needed to energize your team and make necessary changes. While unpleasant at the time, it can be the perfect medicine.

Are you devastated by failure, or do you let it empower you? It's okay to be knocked to the ground and stunned for a while. But eventually, you must get back on your feet, take stock of what happened, and get on with the recovery process.

Expect a Positive Outcome

Positive thoughts have their own energy. It's amazing how they seem to attract positive outcomes. Just the opposite is true of negative thoughts.

Earlier we mentioned Karl Wallenda. Nearly every day of his life, he faced death on the high wire.

During that entire time, he never talked about failure. However, in 1978, at age 73, he fell to his death while performing his high wire act between two skyscrapers in San Juan, Puerto Rico. His wife later told reporters she had worried about her husband that morning because *it was the first time Karl had ever talked about falling before a performance!*

The lesson: If we worry about failure, it can become a self-fulfilling prophecy. It's quite possible that Karl's negative thoughts gave birth to this fatal outcome.

Do you think positive thoughts about the future success of your efforts? Or do you approach a new project with fear and dread? Remember, every day you write the blueprint for success or failure in your subconscious mind. And your mind has an uncanny ability to follow that blueprint.

Dare to Dream of Possibilities

When Michelangelo was asked how he was able to create the Statue of David, he simply said, "I just look at the block of marble and chip away what doesn't belong." In 1961, John F. Kennedy challenged the nation to put a man on the moon before the end of the decade. At that time, the United States hadn't even put a man *in orbit around the Earth*. Martin Luther King dreamed of a time when "men would be judged by the content of their character, rather than the color of their skin." Abraham Lincoln said he could not imagine that a nation could long survive, half slave and half free.

These were men of enormous vision. They weren't daunted by the word, "impossible," but dared to imagine possibilities. Then they inspired us with their vision.

Do you let the label, impossible, prevent you from even making the attempt? Or are you ready to imagine possibilities? Remember, every great achievement began as a vision in someone's mind.

Expand the Box and Explore New Ways

It's been said that the definition of insanity is doing the same thing over and over again and expecting to get a different result. Unless we are willing to take risks and try new things, we will never progress. But what usually happens to the new employee with a novel idea? He's often told, "Oh, that's not the way we do things around here. It would never work. We've always done it this way." Sound familiar?

Let's look at some examples of unconventional thinking (outside the box) that led to breakthroughs. The "Fosbury flop" was an unusual innovation which revolutionized the sport of high jumping. Prior to its introduction, all jumpers went over the bar face first. People scoffed when this new method first appeared—until records were shattered using it! Dr. Edward Deming's idea that "quality is actually less expensive" seemed counter-intuitive at first.

But by eliminating the manufacture of bad products (scrap), great savings were realized. After World War II, the Marshall Plan was an entirely different way of dealing with defeated enemies. We learned our lesson from World War I. Instead of imposing crippling reparations on Germany, Italy, and Japan after the war, *we helped them to rebuild.* Seatbelts were unheard of for much of the automobile's history, but they have since saved countless lives. All of these innovations have led to unprecedented breakthroughs.

What happens to companies that never change and are afraid to look beyond the ideas and methods that give them current success in the marketplace? A study of Fortune 500 companies at ten-year intervals will tell you: Many of the top companies disappeared from the list because they failed to constantly reinvent themselves.

What's your team's attitude toward new ideas? Are they immediately stifled, or listened to and acted upon? Are you a future victim of your present success? Are you constantly on the lookout for the next breakthrough? If the old method isn't working, why not try something else? Open your mind to a novel approach. Change paradigms.

Unfortunately, some companies seem to operate with the attitude, "This would be a great place to work, if it weren't for all those damn customer interruptions." Perhaps a shift to the idea of *customer service* might be in order, *before there are no customers*? If this attitude sounds familiar on your team, you better not wait too long to make the change.

Are you missing out on a breakthrough by sticking to old methods and ways of thinking? Remember, being open to novel ideas is the exact environment you want to cultivate. You can always test a new approach on a small scale first to see if it works. Often, after making a groundbreaking change that totally revitalizes the company, you'll look back and wonder what took you so long.

Keep Moving Forward

Don't rest on your laurels. It's easy to push the coast button and become self satisfied with what you've achieved to date. But that's a recipe for failure.

You were meant to be *in motion*, always progressing, seeking, discovering, exploring, and improving. Standing still to enjoy your reflection in the mirror just makes you susceptible to laziness and arrogance.

The great men and women of history were always on the move. Mother Teresa worked tirelessly among India's poor until the day she died. Major General John Reynolds, one of the most admired officers in the Union Army, was mortally shot from his saddle leading his men at Gettysburg. Morihei Ueshiba, Japan's greatest martial artist, trained daily until his death at 86. They never stopped.

Are you coasting? What have you done to improve yourself lately? What are you contributing to your team? To mankind?

Know When to Compromise

Some people put winning ahead of everything else. They never back off; they never compromise. Their egos rule.

This is idiotic. In any negotiation, Stephen Covey tells us to look for the win-win solution. If a contract doesn't help both parties, then it should be no deal, and both sides can still walk away as friends.

But usually there is some middle ground. *The willingness to look for it* is half the battle. Too often, however, people won't make that effort, so compromise eludes them, to the detriment of both sides. Never compromise if it means abandoning your guiding principles. But if you seek Win-Win, the rewards for both sides can be great indeed.

Do you know when to compromise? Are you willing to give a little to gain a lot?

Pursue "Chudo"

In the martial art of Aikido, "Chudo" means "the middle path, the path of moderation, or just enough." From the writings of Greek philosophers to familiar fairy tales like "Goldie Locks and the Three Bears," it means "just right." For example, when tightening a bolt with a wrench, we can apply too much pressure and break the bolt, or not enough, and fail to tighten it properly. When entering a freeway, there is just the right speed for a safe merge. In landing an airplane, too much flare (pitch up input) will cause the aircraft to stall; not enough might damage the nose gear. In a good conversation there is a balance between listening and speaking.

As a leader, do you apply the golden mean, the proper balance in all your interactions? Are you an *active listener*, or do you monopolize the conversation? Can you play a subordinate role on your team when it's called for, or must you always be *in charge*? Do you ever get out of the way and let junior people gain leadership experience? On your team is it always work, work, work, or do you take some time to have fun together?

"Shodo-O-Seisu"

"Shodo-O-Seisu," or "control the first move" means to be calm, in balance, grounded, and ready with the right attitude. Like an engine idling calmly at an intersection but ready to accelerate, we must be ready to spring into action with efficiency at any time.

For example, don't let a verbal attack throw you off balance. Anticipate what rude or difficult people may say or do ahead of time. Then don't be surprised or let them make you play *their game*. Do your homework well before a meeting; know who will be there and what they might ask. Have a contingency plan. Maintain a non-competitive mindset. Take several deep breaths to settle down when you recognize stress starting to cloud your mind and your response.

Do you control the first move, or let others control you? Be prepared for a possible verbal attack (based on past experience with an individual). But at the same time, don't let that bias your attitude. Give everyone the benefit of the doubt and be open to new behaviors. Over time, eliminate your own hot buttons. That will allow you to remain calm and in control.

"Shoshin-Ni-Kaeru"

"Shoshin-Ni-Kaeru" means "returning to the fundamentals." Sometimes when things seem to be falling apart, it's often because we have strayed from the basics, the underlying guiding principles of our business. That's when it's time to stop and re-evaluate.

In the Navy, when the aircraft accident rate sometimes takes an ominous upward spike, we have a "Safety Standdown." For several days, every squadron in the Navy stops flying and all pilots gather in their ready rooms for an honest self-appraisal. Time-honored safety practices are reviewed, reflected upon, and reinforced. All pilots rededicate themselves to these flying fundamentals. The result is an immediate improvement in safety awareness throughout the Navy and a reduction in the accident rate.

As a company, have you strayed from the fundamentals? Is it time to pause and reflect on those *guiding principles* that brought you success in the past? When was the last time you had a company-wide training day? When was the last time senior managers took a leadership retreat together? Or maybe it's time to have a Family Appreciation Day to remind ourselves that it's not all about work.

Strive for "Dochu-No-Sei"

"Dochu-No-Sei" means "calmness in action." We are much more capable of handling adversity when we remain calm. A nervous tennis player double faults; a panicked golfer, in a sudden death playoff with a relaxed Tiger Woods, slices his drive into the rough. On the other hand, Michael Jordan, with the game on the line, takes the last shot and usually makes it, because he's not worried about missing.

Many of the great battles in history were won by calm, steady leadership in the face of dire circumstances that would make lesser men panic. Seeing General Robert E. Lee, astride his horse, Traveler, inspired his men to be courageous, despite the carnage all around them. General Lee often rode to the front of the battle when the outcome was in doubt—only to be led away by his men, fearful of losing their beloved leader, with the cry, "Lee to the rear." The mere presence of this courageous leader on the battlefield often provided the margin of victory. Lee was steadfast, the eye of the hurricane for his men.

As a leader, are you aware that subordinates take their cues from you, watching your every move? What image do you project when things are going to hell in a hand basket? Do you instill calm? Or do you panic and spread chaos among those you lead?

IV

Leave a Legacy and a Legion of Future Leaders

Emphasize Character, Not Personality

To celebrate America's bicentennial in 1976, Dr. Stephen Covey was asked to do a study of leadership covering all that had been written on the subject during the first 200 years of our nation's history. After the research was completed, he made a remarkable observation. In the leadership literature of the first 150 years, the writings emphasized the importance of *character* in our leaders. In the last 50 years the emphasis shifted to *personality*. Is it possible we have gotten off the track by emphasizing the wrong thing?

Personality is but the tip of the iceberg in a leader. What's much more important is character, the nine-tenths that lies below the surface. Take a look at history. Abraham Lincoln and George Washington had uniquely different personalities. So did Patton and Bradley, Grant and Lee. *But what they all had in common was great character*. That was the bedrock of their leadership. Each possessed an unerring moral compass. They had uncompromising value systems with strong beliefs in integrity, courage, teamwork, and self-sacrifice.

What is the foundation for your own leadership? Is it superficial: personality and a desire to be popular? Or is it something much deeper: *character and respect*?

Let Your Spirit Shine

It is said that Mother Teresa lit up a room by her mere presence. Her spirit touched everyone around her.

We've all felt the influence of charismatic people. It's something we've experienced at an intangible level, not easily defined, but real nonetheless. Abraham Lincoln, Robert E. Lee, Martin Luther King, and Gandhi all had this undeniable power. What is it about them that projected such an aura?

Simply, it is a lifetime of selfless sacrifice and devotion to others that builds a spirit of such immense power. Throughout their lives, they remained true to their guiding principles, which enabled them to uplift and inspire everyone they met. Their characters, polished through years of good works, shine like beacons, even today, long after they have died.

Does your spirit shine like a beacon? Are you building character that will influence others for years to come? What will your legacy be?

Seek "Masa-Katsu-Agatsu"

"Masa-Katsu-Agatsu" means "True victory is victory over yourself."

Many people spend an entire lifetime trying to control others: what they think, what they do, and what they say. It is a futile effort, guaranteeing only frustration. Your time is better spent working on yourself. Master yourself and you can be a powerful influence on others.

How do you achieve self-mastery? Start by listing ten improvements you want to make in the next year. Every night, make an honest assessment of how you did *that day*. Don't beat yourself up. This self-appraisal must be detached and objective, *free from blame or criticism*. Approach it with the attitude of a scientist who merely remarks, "That's interesting."

Follow Benjamin Franklin's example by trying to make small, incremental improvements every day. Over time, you'll be amazed. By harnessing your *intent* to change, together with an objective, daily self-appraisal, you'll begin to witness a transformation. In a sense, you start with a vision of the person you wish to become, then slowly become that person.

It takes years of patience and painstaking effort, and a willingness to endure lapses and setbacks. But in the end, it will all be worth it because the direct benefactor is *you*. It's not easy, but it works. Remember, Benjamin Franklin successfully used this method over an entire lifetime.

As a leader, do you waste time trying to change others but invest little time working on yourself? What's stopping you from beginning to change *today*? Is it because you expect instant results and don't have the patience? Or do you feel the road is too long to even begin? Just remember the old proverb, "The journey of 1000 miles begins with the first step."

Steer by Your Stars

Every leader, like the mariners of old, needs stars to steer by. Every action and every decision must be based on these guiding principles.

Lou Holtz, the football coach at Notre Dame for many years, measured his actions by just three things:

1. Do your best.
2. Do what is right.
3. Treat others the way you want to be treated.

If he followed these principles at all times, he knew he was on the right track, whether he won or lost. In fact, Lou would say that *losing* was really *learning*.

What are your guiding principles? What do you stand for? Have you written them down where you can see them and review them often? Do they guide all of your actions and decisions?

Believe in the "Spirit" of Leadership

"Spirit" concerns the intangibles of leadership, those things that civilizations throughout the ages have always valued such as honor, courage, commitment, truth, loyalty, friendship, family, goodness, respect, and an acknowledgement of a Higher Power.

Our Founding Fathers were deeply aware of these

intangibles. For example, while they were against a single, state-mandated religion, they certainly had no intention of removing all things of the spirit from this new experiment called the United States of America. They knew that spirit was already deeply embedded in colonial culture. They ensured it was written into our Declaration of Independence and our Constitution ("...endowed by their Creator with certain, inalienable rights, among them life, liberty, and the pursuit of happiness.").

Spirit made the American Revolution a worthy cause. It was the foundation of Lincoln's leadership during the dark days of the Civil War. Even today, we still print "In God We Trust" on our money and open each session of Congress with a prayer. Our elected officials and people giving testimony in a court of law swear an oath on the Bible. Spirit is as relevant today as it was then.

Do you ignore the power of spirit in your leadership? Do you avoid it because it's the "soft" side of leadership, in other words, too "touchy-feely"? Do you fail to realize that *working with people is all "soft stuff"*? Or do you deny this dimension in yourself out of embarrassment, because it's too private, or because you want to be politically correct? If so, your leadership will lack true depth.

Act According to Your Conscience

Every one of us has a little voice deep inside called conscience that never lies to us; it is brutally honest. It lets us know if what we're doing is morally right. It critiques our every move. We can choose not to listen, but it is still undeniably there.

It is a powerful aid to great leaders when they follow it. It gives moral resonance to their decisions. We frequently wrestle with it, try to rationalize with it, or outright ignore it and stifle it. But conscience is very resilient, and keeps telling us the truth, whether we listen or not.

Nothing good ever seems to come when we stray from the advice of this most subtle voice within. But over time, if we ignore it too often, its voice may become too weak to be heard anymore.

As a leader, have you lost your most important ally, conscience? Without a moral compass, do you think good leadership is even possible? History shows us the horrifying consequences of powerful leaders who acted without this moral compass: Hitler, Stalin, Nero, Tojo, and Mussolini to name just a few. In contrast to their great evil, we have moral leaders such as Lincoln, Gandhi, Washington, and Martin Luther King.

Who serves as *your* role model? As a leader, do you ever use dirty tricks to get an edge or make the deal? To get that coveted promotion do you abandon ethics? Do you encourage salesmen on your staff to make their quotas using questionable and deceptive methods? Don't be fooled. Even though unethical tactics may seem to provide a competitive edge, the hubris and dishonesty of companies like Enron lead to disaster.

Recognize a Higher Power

If you think you can manage to get through life on your own without any help, you're sadly mistaken. Whether you're a Zen Buddhist, American Indian who worships "The Great Spirit," Taoist, Muslim, Hindu, Jew, or Christian, most people somehow realize that there is a Higher Power at work among us. All cultures, throughout history, have been drawn to their own concept of a Supreme Being. It's an awareness built into our human nature. It ties us all together.

We may pretend that God doesn't exist, but the evidence to the contrary is overwhelming. One look at Nature tells us the world is not some random event. All of this order and design is, without a doubt, the work of a *Grand Architect*. To deny his existence would be like saying you could take all the parts of a Chevy truck, put them in a large box, give them an infinite amount of shaking, and eventually see a fully assembled vehicle. It's just not going to happen!

Despite the denial of a minority of atheists and agnostics, it should comfort us that God, however we choose to know him, does indeed exist. He is there to help us. All we have to do is ask. While he doesn't necessarily answer our prayers in the way we expect, *he does answer them all, in his own way and in his own time*.

As a leader, do you acknowledge a higher power? Do you let him guide you? A deep and abiding faith in the Almighty is your most powerful resource.

Don't Seek Earthly Rewards

Sad and empty is the man who spends his whole life accumulating material wealth. In Charles Dickens's *A Christmas Carol*, Ebenezer Scrooge sees his possible fate: His possessions become links in a heavy chain, which he fashions around his own neck, to be hauled around for all eternity, just like his former partner, Jacob Marley.

Did you ever notice how the rich and famous are often the most unhappy and unfulfilled? Each extravagant purchase they make gives only temporary pleasure. Soon they are seeking something bigger and better—bigger car, bigger boat, bigger house, bigger airplane. But that only perpetuates the cycle, leaving them frustrated once again. Contrast them to Mother Teresa, who spent a lifetime of service to the "poorest of the poor." She lacked earthly possessions, but radiated joy and happiness.

In the end, we will be judged by the size of our heart, not the size of our bank account. Whoever said "you can't take it with you" and "the best things in life are free" was absolutely right.

Are you fashioning your own chain of earthly possessions like Ebenezer Scrooge? Do you equate money with success? Do you judge people by the cars they drive, where they live, or their titles? Do you think you can ever *buy* true happiness?

"To Thine Own Self Be True…"

Shakespeare told us, "To thine own self be true, and it follows as the night the day, that thou cannot then be false to any man."

Many of our problems begin with kidding *ourselves*. We pretend we are something we're not, make phony excuses to ourselves, or rationalize our own behavior. It all boils down to pride and ego. We are reluctant to look at our true selves, because deep down inside, we know we are lacking in many qualities we wish we had. And we certainly don't want others to discover our secret.

But that *brutally honest* self-appraisal is just what we need for true growth. It's a starting point. It will allow us to become the individuals we would really like to be. When we are honest with ourselves, we no longer have to play games with other people. We cast off the burden of trying to be someone we're not. We can then begin the lifelong task of daily self-improvement.

Do you know who you really are? Do you have

the courage to make an honest self-appraisal, in spite of what you may discover? Do you realize that, while painful, this can be very liberating and lead to great personal growth?

Spread the Light

All of us are on earth for a purpose, each with certain talents. For some, that may be the ability to create magnificent works of art: the Statue of David, the Mona Lisa, the Pieta. For others, it may be the ability to design and build architectural wonders: the Taj Mahal, Saint Peter's Basilica, the Great Pyramid, the Temple of Jerusalem. Still others, such as Mozart, Chopin, and Beethoven, may have the gift of music. Could anyone doubt for a moment that all these amazing abilities were gifts, something they were born with?

But the ability to lead and motivate people is also a gift. Everyone has it to a certain degree. However, certain men and women throughout history have had this talent in abundance: Moses, Alexander the Great, Abraham Lincoln, Robert E. Lee, and Margaret Thatcher, to name a few. They stand out in their ability to lead and influence others.

We get into trouble, however, when we start thinking of ourselves as the source of any of these inborn talents. Like the lighthouses of old that guarded rocky shores, each had a brilliant source of light, a bright flame if you will. But that illuminating light is *not our own*. We can only be mirrors, reflecting that light to the far horizon. *We can polish the mirror, but we are never the flame.*

So what is our role in life? Isn't it taking the gifts that have been given to us, polishing the mirror, and spreading the light as far as possible?

Now that you have read *my* reflections, ask yourself this critical question:

What strategies of great leadership will you leave as YOUR legacy?

It will make all the difference in the world!

Appendix
Guiding Principles

Every leader, like the mariners of old, needs stars to steer by. Every action and every decision must be based on these Guiding Principles.

What are your Guiding Principles? What do you stand for? Have you written them down where you can see them and review them often? Do they guide all of your actions and decisions?

You won't always measure up to your Guiding Principles, but they are there to help you get back on course.

Everyone needs to create his or her own Guiding Principles, but as an example, the next page shows the eleven stars I steer by, designed for display on a single page.

GUIDING PRINCIPLES

- Continually develop own character traits to be able to inspire others. Set the example.
- See failure for what it really is: a great chance for growth and learning.
- Lift up everyone you meet.
- Never overlook the value of a sense of humor.
- Learn from everyone you meet.
- Use stories and analogies to communicate.
- Take time to reflect.
- Listen.
- "To thine own self be true..."
- Don't be afraid to say, "I'm sorry," or, "I was wrong." You're human.
- Have the courage to follow God's plan for you.

Here is a more detailed explanation of what those Guiding Principles mean:

1. **Continually develop own character traits to be able to inspire others. Set the example.** You are always a "work in progress" trying to make small improvements every day. And nothing is more important for you as a leader than setting the example.

2. **See failure for what it really is: a great chance for growth and learning.** Use mistakes as stepping stones to ultimate success. None of mankind's greatest achievements was ever realized without a lot of mistakes being made along the way.

3. **Lift up everyone you meet.** Everyone who encounters you should be better off for the experience.

4. **Never overlook the value of a sense of humor.** The ability to laugh at yourself and your own mistakes is critical to your team's success. Humor has the power to defuse the most difficult situations.

5. **Learn from everyone you meet.** Every person you meet is smarter than you are in some way, often in many ways. Know when to be a teacher and when to be a student. It keeps you humble.

6. **Use stories and analogies to communicate.** Many of our best leaders were great story tellers. Don't overlook this great way to communicate.

Leave a Legacy

7. **Take time to reflect.** Pause each day to unwind and reflect on your Guiding Principles and the goals of your team.

8. **Listen.** The Good Lord gave us two ears and one mouth. Maybe that should tell us something about the ratio of listening to speaking. Stephen Covey tells us that an empathetic listener "seeks to understand before being understood."

9. **"To thine own self be true..."** Shakespeare said it best. If you are true to yourself, you can't be false to any man.

10. **Don't be afraid to say, "I'm sorry," or, "I was wrong." You're human.** You're going to make mistakes because you're human. Be ready to make a sincere apology.

11. **Have the courage to follow God's plan for you.** God has a plan for each and every one of us. Have the courage to follow it.

Your Guiding Principles can also help you create your own "Leadership Philosophy." It's important that you communicate this to your team early and often. They need to know what you stand for—and won't stand for! Mine starts on the next page.

Leadership Philosophy

I will follow the Golden Rule and always treat others the way I wish to be treated. I will treat others with the dignity, decency, and respect they deserve as fellow human beings.

I will follow my conscience and always strive to do what is right, regardless of the consequences or the personal price I may have to pay. I will always lead others with fairness and consistency.

I will be a Servant Leader, always putting others before myself.

I will lead others by my example, always trying to give my best effort in anything I do. I will continually develop my own character in order to inspire others.

I will see failure for what it really is: a great chance for growth and learning. I will use mistakes only to teach myself and others, never for self-criticism, regret, or worry.

I will lift up everyone I meet. I want anyone who meets me to be better off for the experience. I will empower others to achieve their full potential.

I will maintain my sense of humor and use it to defuse tense or stressful situations. I will retain the ability to laugh at myself.

I will value growth and learning and remember that everyone I meet has something to teach me.

I will use stories and analogies to communicate, knowing that this is the way the great leaders of history have reached others.

I will take time to listen and then reflect on what I have heard without jumping to conclusions.

I will always be true to myself and never lie to myself or others.

I won't be afraid to say, "I'm sorry," or, "I was wrong," because I am human. I will strive to be tolerant of others.

I will have the courage to follow God's plan for me, knowing that His way, not mine, is always better. I will rely on God and remember that great leadership is impossible without His help.

Name Index

A

Aesop 83
Alexander the Great 18, 122

B

Omar Bradley 113

C

Neville Chamberlain 56
Winston Churchill 31, 91
Hernando Cortez 99
Stephen Covey 80, 106, 113, 127
George Armstrong Custer 85

D

David 84, 102
Edward Deming 103
Charles Dickens 120
John Donne 13, 51, 52, 69
Dr. Wayne Dyer 44

E

Thomas Edison 28, 97
Loren Eiseley 59
Dwight Eisenhower 33

F

Henry Ford 69, 82
Dick Fosbury 103
Ben Franklin 31

G

Mahatma Gandhi 18, 24, 114, 118
Goliath 84
Forrest Gregg 87

H

Hannibal 18
George Herbert 61
Thomas Herndon 31
Adolf Hitler 56, 66, 92, 118
Lou Holtz 74, 116
Robert Horry 90

I

Lee Iacocca 81, 91
Judas Iscariot 53

J

Jesus 18, 24, 52, 55, 83
John Paul II 18
Andrew Johnson 59
Michael Jordan 109

K

John F. Kennedy 13, 18, 31, 59, 82, 102
Martin Luther King, Jr. 13, 18, 60, 102, 114, 118
Jerry Kramer 87

L

Robert E. Lee 13, 18, 109, 114, 122
Abraham Lincoln 13, 18, 31, 60, 66, 83, 102, 113, 114, 122
Vince Lombardi 87

M

Mickey Mantle 74

Jacob Marley 120
George Marshall 104
Michelangelo 102
Dennis Miller 24
Moses 122
Benito Mussolini 118

N

Nero 118

P

Rosa Parks 60
George Patton 34, 113
Saint Paul 52

R

Ronald Reagan 18
John Reynolds 105
Teddy Roosevelt 18, 86
Babe Ruth 89

S

Pete Sampras 90
King Saul 84
Ebenezer Scrooge 120, 121
William Shakespeare 121, 127
Josef Stalin 118
Leland Stanford 54
Picabo Street 88, 94

T

Mother Teresa 13, 18, 24, 105, 114, 120
Margaret Thatcher 122
Tojo 118

U

Morihei Ueshiba 47, 105
Johnny Unitas 26

W

Karl Wallenda 98, 101
George Washington 18, 60, 113, 118
John Wooden 9, 11, 13, 18
Tiger Woods 109

ABOUT THE AUTHOR

Captain Stew Fisher is a cum laude graduate of the U.S. Naval Academy at Annapolis. He retired from the Navy in 1998 after 31 years of service spanning the Vietnam War and Desert Storm.

Captain Fisher led the Navy's first Blackhawk helicopter combat search and rescue squadron in Desert Storm, working with Navy SEAL teams, and later commanded 2000 men and women at Naval Air Stations Pt. Mugu, Lemoore, and China Lake, California. Awards received include the Air Medal, Presidential Unit Citation, Legion of Merit, and the Meritorious Service Medal.

During his long career, he attended the Industrial College of the Armed Forces in Washington, D.C., and served in the Secretary of the Navy's Total Quality Leadership Office. He authored and taught many of the Navy's quality and leadership courses and was a Strategic Planning Instructor/Facilitator.

In his civilian career, Stew has served as an ISO 9000 auditor. He has developed "The Lighthouse: Advanced Leadership Seminar" which explores the secrets of great leaders, past and present.

Stew is also a black belt in the martial art of Aikido and is a certified FAA Flight Instructor in both helicopter and fixed-wing aircraft.

Stew lives in Camarillo, California, and Trenton, Michigan, with his wife, Yolanda. They have seven grown children and one grandchild: Molly, Kelly, Patrick, John, Jason, Renee, Shawn, and Christopher.

Stew teaches a two-day leadership seminar, "The Lighthouse," based on the principles found in his three books and is available for coaching your team. You can contact him at Tqlmstr@aol.com.

Buy more great reads from this author and others by
visiting our online catalog at
http://www.signalmanpublishing.com

www.ingramcontent.com/pod-product-compliance
Lightning Source LLC
LaVergne TN
LVHW021349080426
835508LV00020B/2186